RECLAIM YOUR AUTHOR CAREER

USING THE ENNEAGRAM TO BUILD YOUR STRATEGY, UNLOCK DEEPER PURPOSE, AND CELEBRATE YOUR CAREER

CLAIRE TAYLOR

www.ffs.media

Author photograph by Anna Monette

CONTENTS

CHAPTER 1
IS THIS BOOK FOR ME?

ARE YOU READY?

Do you ever feel like your writing business is burning more fuel than it should? Like you're wasting precious energy on things that don't move you forward, but you're not sure what those things are?

What matters? What doesn't? It's not easy to sort through.

What you can expect in the pages ahead is a transformational process, a new way of relating to your writing, and a fresh perspective on the industry. You'll also gain an updated and individualized set of criteria for making the important decisions a business owner must—both big and small.

But as it is with all transformation and growth, discomfort, honesty, and sweat equity are a necessary part of the bargain. I promise this to you: you will get just as much out of this book as you put in.

From day one, my goal in writing this book has been to design something that will change your entire career for the better, so that your natural energy and enthusiasm can flow through the mechanisms of your business unimpeded and unwasted.

This book might feel like author boot camp at times, but unlike boot camp, the goal isn't to enforce conformity, but rather to encourage and embolden your individual center, the part of you that society tries to buff out and erase, that little voice that may be quite hoarse lately from trying to shout over the noise. And we'll create that alignment between your career and your deepest self by using a tool called the Enneagram.

Life is crazy. You probably have a lot going on outside of your writing life.

Or maybe you don't. Maybe writing has *become* your life because you thought that was the only way to cross the illustrious Finish Line of Success. But you *could* have a life outside of writing, if you wanted to, and a legendary one at that. The myth that you must forfeit everything outside of your work to be a successful writer, like some obsessed Stephen King protagonist (and doesn't that always work well for them?) is one of the many myths I'll gladly dispel for you in the following pages.

I'll show you that, in fact, your creative work *suffers* when you have nothing else going on outside of it—no exterior stimulation, no personal challenges, no new input. Living your life is part of your work.

You deserve to be a full-spectrum person who feels successful in your writing and earns the money that you need to remain an active member of this industry, whatever amount that is for you.

It sounds like a tall order, I know. If you're a skeptic like I am, you're probably thinking I might as well promise you that for the price of this book I can make your wildest dreams come true. Or maybe you're reading these words and going, "Oh wow, is this going to be an extended sales pitch for a higher-priced item?"

That would be smart of me to do if I cared more about money than my integrity, but I don't, so that's not what this is. I do offer paid courses and services, but my goal is to make this book something where you walk away with way more than your money's worth. If you choose to work with me more in the future, great! We can have some serious fun together! But it's not required to take something valuable away from this.

Reclaim Your Author Career is, at its heart, an empowerment book. I want you to know *how* to make the many decisions you face in this business so that you don't need to ask someone like me what to do at every crossroad. Outside perspective can be invaluable, but the more decisions you can confidently make for yourself going forward, the better, right?

That's my goal in writing this book. Ready to see if we can pull it off?

WHO AM I?

You may or may not know who the hell I am. So here are the highlights (and lowlights):

First and foremost, I'm a writer. A humor writer, at that; I picked an uphill battle for myself when it comes to selling books. Second to being a writer, I'm a reader, and that's important because, thirdly, I'm a story consultant. I call myself a "fiction strategist" because the approach I take to helping authors with their stories tends to go so much deeper than just the book itself. You'll see that as you progress through these chapters.

Before I was a full-time writer, I was an editor and a teacher. That probably makes me sound stuffy, but I promise I was never the type to dock points from the essay for spelling. I'm more of an idea junkie.

Story is my obsession. I've edited over two hundred fiction manuscripts. I read fifty to a hundred books a year in all different genres, including fiction and nonfiction. I've published somewhere around thirty-five books in the sundry genres of religious satire, paranormal police comedy, magical cozy mystery, and crime fiction (and erotica, but I don't talk about that in "mixed company"). Story is my breakfast, lunch, and dinner. (Not my dessert, though. I prefer ice cream.)

When you're passionate about something, you want to share that passion with others. So, in a way, I was destined/doomed for teaching. Both of my parents are teachers, and one time on a paranormal research trip to New Orleans, I had a psychic tell me there was a ton of blue "teaching" energy flying around my aura. Like I said, destined/doomed.

I can't think of any career more in alignment with who I am and what I'm passionate about than writing meaningful stories and helping other authors do the same.

MY MISALIGNMENT TALE

What's so great about alignment, you might ask? How about I answer that by telling what's so bad about misalignment?

When I began writing full-time, I didn't take the leap because I was suddenly making enough money to replace my previous income. I took the leap because my last job was a nightmare, and I knew I had to get out. I needed money fast from writing, so I tried a lot of get-rich-quick schemes. Nothing unethical, but definitely unrealistic. This was back in 2015, so it wasn't exactly the Kindle golden years, but there was still a good bit of money to rake in from Kindle Unlimited without much advertising at all.

So, that's the path I took. Because, you know, I needed *money*.

Fair enough, 2015 Claire.

The problem, of course—and you'll probably see this from miles away—was that I was focused *entirely* on money. This is not unexpected behavior when someone goes from having a paycheck to not having one. However, it's not ideal. My thinking was, *I need money, and I finally have time to pursue my passion of writing and my dream of being a writer, so let's find the easiest overlap and go, go, go!*

I was younger, coming out of a high-stress, low-paying job in public education, and never doubted for a second my ability to white-knuckle my life. I could do this! I could make back my old salary in book sales!

Prior to teaching, I'd worked as an in-house editor for a romance publisher, so I was at least able to rely on those skills to pick up freelance jobs and pay the bills. But I wanted to be a *writer*. I wanted my income to come from *writing*. My identity would settle for nothing less. And because of that, I wrote a lot of words that I didn't care that much about, until fulfilling my childhood dream of being a writer became an unfulfilling slog. And then I hit a big fucking wall.

One of the most important characteristics to remember about walls is that they hurt to run headlong into. That's not the *only* important thing about them, but it's the important thing for our purposes.

My options were to either pivot or to keep running into that mental and emotional wall. Eventually, and I mean *eventually*, I chose pivoting (I am incredibly stubborn), and while it felt demoralizing to start from square one again with a different pen name but in a genre I actually cared about, it was the right choice. I can say with confidence that it's proven to be the best one in the long run.

In reading this book, you may come to the conclusion that you, too, want to pivot. A pivot costs time and money—there's just no getting around that—and not all pivots will be equally beneficial for you. So you'll want to make sure that you pivot in the *right* direction the first time. That motion of repetitive pivoting is the same silly walk that you see from tourists on a busy street who don't know where they're going. And when you don't know where you're going, you end up wasting a lot of time taking wrong turns, circling around, backtracking, and pretending you meant to head that way the whole time.

That's all energy that you could spend with your friends. Or if you don't have friends anymore because you've been ignoring them (hey, it happens!), that's energy you can spend making new friends. It's energy you could spend with your spouse, with your kids, on hobbies, travel, volunteering, getting a massage, learning a new language, showing your spouse for the thousandth time how to properly fold your shirts, starting a delicious blood feud with your neighbors that will span generations, voting, researching who you should vote for before you go and vote, having sex, playing soccer, makeup tutorial videos, cleaning under the fridge, writing jokes, training your dogs to fetch you a beer, or sharing your favorite album with your kids.

More succinctly, sources of potential fast cash pop up all the time, and if you follow those, your life will become a nonstop pivot party. I speak from personal experience when I say that's not a gathering you want to attend.

WHO IS THIS BOOK FOR?

I don't mean to be facetious, but if you picked up this book based on the title, this book is for you. If you feel out of whack, then this book is for you. If you've never seriously considered what it means to have an aligned career, then this book is definitely for you (and expect to feel a little bit pissed off as you read it, because that's what happens when we start the alignment process: we get a little bit pissed off, and we feel huge relief, all at the same time).

If you already know everything there is to know about alignment, why did you pick up this book? Doesn't matter. This book is still for you. If nothing else, we can all use an occasional reminder of the things we already know. Especially when that thing we know is something that society has told us to forget, something we've been discouraged from even considering for ourselves.

Almost every institution we encounter in our life rewards us for fitting in. School, sports, the corporate world—they each come with predetermined, impersonal metrics for success and failure, which isn't *all* bad but deprives us of the opportunity to define those things for ourselves. Because of that, we can waste a lot of energy on fitting in or conforming to expectations, energy that would be better spent toward a purpose that deeply moves us from the inside out. Some call this "internal motivation."

Back to whether or not this book is for you.

The unavoidable reality is that the people who stand to benefit the most from this book will suffer the strongest adverse reaction to it. That's because we're going to dive into what connects us deeply to ourselves and others, and when we talk about that we must also inevitably address what in our past and present is causing us to disconnect from ourselves and others. We're going to talk about self-worth, safety, power, and so many more sensitive concepts that, taken out of context, could make me a trending topic on Twitter. So this book may feel a little bit like therapy, but it's a hell of a lot cheaper.

And last, but certainly not least, to get the most out of this book, you should be an author. By an "author," I mean you are a creative type and want to tell stories. Ideally, you'll specifically be an "independent author" and in charge of which stories you tell and how. That doesn't mean that this isn't applicable to those who take the traditional publishing route of finding an agent who hooks you up with a publisher, only that when you do that—when you establish the artificial gatekeeper of not only an agent but a publisher—your idea of success and your creative values may not be appreciated by those few people who get to tell you yes or no. In a traditional publishing setting, you will undoubtedly find yourself, yet again, required to conform to impersonal standards and metrics. And with that restriction comes the question of "What am I willing to sacrifice of myself so that my vision, in its incomplete form, can be seen?"

You may even find that your desire to be traditionally published doesn't align with your core motivations. If that's the case, congratulations! You're free to take matters into your own hands and publish independently. Welcome to the club!

It's this opportunity for true alignment that makes me love the indie author lifestyle so much. Because once you know who you are as a storyteller and what you want to accomplish, there is no one you must sacrifice your sense of purpose and trajectory to appease.

If that sounds enticing, I'm happy to say this book is for you.

FINDING YOUR GUIDING STAR

The indie author community is my home. The people I talk to every day, the friends I can confide my hopes, dreams, and fears to, are often indie authors. I have plenty of friends outside of writing, but because none of them can fathom my career, I don't bother talking with them about the thing that absorbs most of my waking hours. For many of us, writing has turned from a passion to a business to a lifestyle, so when I see something toxic creeping into the industry, I take it personally. Thwarting it becomes all I can think about.

(This can be traced directly back to my Enneagram type, but more on that later.)

Have you ever had this interaction?

THEM: What do you do for work?

YOU: I'm a writer.

For so many of us, writing becomes not just what we *do*, but who we *are*. This is not the ideal approach for a balanced life, but it's the reality for most of us, so until we shake it, we must learn to navigate it and do the best we can with it. We can worry about relegating writing from our identity to one of the many verbs in our lives later, but for now, we need to see clearly how much it seeps into our self-perception to understand how crucial it is to take the reins on that identity.

That's why it's so important to get a clear vision of what you want and why you want it before you charge in. If your writing has become your life, then by reclaiming your author career, you'll reclaim your life along with it.

And it's also why this book exists. As the indie publishing industry matures, the cracks begin to show. The center of the most successful marketing tactics today will not hold. Your career will have twists and turns and necessary failures, and if you don't have a clear sense of purpose as a guiding star by which to orient yourself, you won't make it through.

Take, for example, the rapid release tactic, where you publish a book every month or two, which supposedly earns you favor with the Amazon Algorithm of Lore. This tactic has served a lot of indies well, financially speaking, for the last few years. But there is a big difference between the six books a year that one had to publish back in 2016 to keep up and the roughly six thousand one must publish annually for it to have a reliable effect today. For every indie it has made rich, that relentless grind has burned out fifty more.

I would know. I was one of the burnouts back in 2018.

There's got to be another way, right? Even if you're publishing at a more comfortable four books a year, do you really want to do that for the rest of your life? Or do you want to create stories that connect so deeply with readers that they won't forget you, that they'll keep recommending your books to their friends, who will recommend them to *their* friends, and so on until the friends of friends of friends pass them down to their children?

Those are the kinds of books that make a career. *Good Omens, The Princess Bride, Interview with the Vampire, A Wrinkle in Time*—all "genre fiction" that has endured. And guess what? Writing a book that resonates like these classics doesn't have to take years of your life. You just need clarity on a few important elements (that we'll discuss) to allow the story to flow from you in a natural and meaningful way. And when the right readers find it, they will want to tell the world.

I believe this is what most authors dream of when they set out in this career. We want to write stories that challenge, comfort, transform, inspire, and motivate our readers. We want to do something great, something altruistic.

And then money gets involved, which is often necessary but always so, so complicated.

MOTIVATION

This is a book about motivation. It's a book about what motivates your protagonist, what motivates your reader, and, most importantly, what motivates you. So, in effect, what you learn from this is more about yourself and the world around you. It will translate to much more than just your author career, and that's great. That's what I call a bonus. But I'm going to keep relating it back to you, your readers, and your characters.

We're going to discuss the different *kinds* of motivations and the effects of each. Specifically, we'll talk about fears and desires. There are a lot of things that are widely feared and widely desired, and each of those things will motivate most people a little bit. But that's not good enough for me, and I think you'll find that that's not good enough for you in the long term either.

For instance, we're all motivated to a various extent by money. Money is good. I like money. Apparently, I have to say that up front because when I talk about what it is I talk about in this book, people come at me with: "Why do you hate money?" and "What's wrong with wanting to make money? I have to support my family. Do you have to support your family? Do you even have a family? Are you even lovable? I have my doubts because of the way you talk about money."

If there was a font to denote that someone's hackles were raised, I would've used it just then.

Listen, I was not kidding when I said that this book will piss off some people, because I'm going to question traditional ideas. We're going to knock over some sandcastles that you've built over the course of your life so that you can replace them with something that will withstand the tide.

So, yes, we *all* like money. We desire it. That's great. But *why* do you desire it?

Everyone wants money to *do* something for them on an emotional level. There are incentives that motivate all of us a little bit, like the promise of easy money or social status, but when that little bit runs out or takes too long to get or doesn't fulfill us the way we'd imagined, what are we left with?

What we will be looking at here, the foundation upon which we will be aligning our indie author careers moving forward, is not generic motivation, but the fear and desire that lies at the core of each of us.

Spoiler alert: it's not the same for everyone. But also, no one's is truly unique. And that affords us the opportunity to categorize a finite number of core motivations that will allow us to view them and say, "Yes, *that* is the core motivation behind everything I do in this profession." And once that is identified, then we build out from there. We align everything from that starting point, that true north.

You will learn what that point is for you, for your protagonist, and for your ideal reader. Once you master this, you will be a fear- and desire-regulating queen. You will know exactly how to motivate your characters to do what you need them to do, how to give your readers the perfect balance of light and dark that resonates with them, and how to write stories that allow you to confront and indulge your fears and desires in such a way that storytelling becomes an arena of personal exploration and fulfillment like you've never experienced.

"That's all well and good, Claire, but I wanna do this professionally. I want to make *money*. You haven't even talked about money yet."

Oh, but I have. *waggles eyebrows* Because when you know your audience, and you know what they want, you can also guess where they're hanging out, and how to deliver a satisfying story—a "product," if you want to be crass—that they will buy every single time.

Alignment is the path to loyal fans, and loyal fans build sustainable careers. They also build lucrative ones over time.

What we're doing is deconstructing your indie author career, and rather than starting from the question of "How do I make money from my work?" we start from the point of "What kind of work do I want to make money from?" Only then do we address the second question of "How do I make money from it?"

Those are the questions that we will ask and answer over the course of this book.

OUR APPROACH

We're going to examine your indie author career in a specific way. I like to picture it as concentric circles.

Not to be too presumptuous, but I'm gonna throw this out there: you are a person.

Your career is a part of you being a person. So when we talk about your indie author career, we're not talking about you *entirely*, we're talking about a *part* of you that is your career. It's crucial to remember that our career is only a part of us.

Making up this career are four concentric circles. The outermost is your creative values. And I know that term seems vague right now, because it is. But don't worry, there's a whole chapter on it and we're going to go in depth into it (it's the chapter where you're most likely to shake your fist angrily at the heavens and curse my name).

Now, your creative values, once established, will inform your author persona—that is, the person you present to the world, the writer. So, the next circle down, nestled inside career values, represents your persona. To some extent, every reader is aware that someone has written the story they are reading, and that becomes an element of the story itself. In a time of so many people publishing, and with so many stories hitting the same tropes (*not* a bad thing), you want to differentiate yourself, the author, because that is something that no one else can truly mimic when it's authentic. It is something you can bring to the table that will connect with readers in a world that is the most connected and the most disconnected it's ever been. So, while this element of an indie author career is often overlooked, it absolutely should not be. Persona is a secret weapon.

And then, the next circle down, within persona, is our themes. Oh sweet mother of pearl, I will go into detail on theme and why your story absolutely must have one. If you ever see me after hours at a conference with a drink in my hand, and you're wondering the fastest way to get me to cause a scene, simply say these words: "Stories do not need to have themes." Clearly, they do, and there's a crucial emotional reason why. I'll go into that later like a district attorney with election on the line at the murder trial of the century. (I watch a lot of true crime, and I'm not afraid to use it.) Theme is the bedrock of story.

And lastly, the smallest of these concentric circles represents your story's protagonist. We align the protagonist with the theme in which that protagonist operates so the two resonate beautifully and seamlessly, creating optimal internal conflict, which paves the way for a satisfying resolution to that conflict. We also align those two elements within the context of your author persona, the way you present yourself to the world as "writer" and the voice and brain and heart behind the words your readers love. We nestle all of this nicely within the creative values that inspire you and bring you that crucial sense of purpose within your career, so that you can't wait to sit down and work.

All of this is constructed *based on you* rather than to appease a mold created by society during the Industrial Revolution.

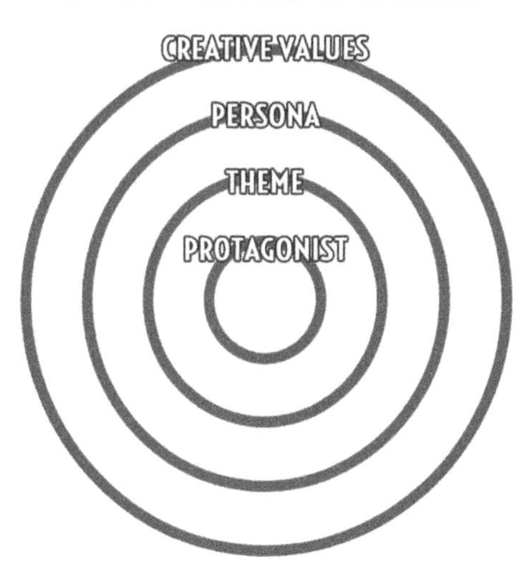

That may sound like a tall order, and it is, but I love tall orders. It helps that I know exactly the right tool to use to make sure you get the precise alignment of these elements that will sustain you over the many, many years of your career. It's a little thing called the Enneagram.

For the uninitiated, don't worry, we go way into this tool in chapter 1. And if you already know what the Enneagram is, isn't this exciting? I'm excited.

WHY DO I BOTHER?

The writer in me knows how necessary it is to build a strong foundation for your career. The reader in me craves more timeless stories. The editor in me wants you to dig deeper, find that brilliance, and polish it until it shines. And the teacher in me wants to show as many people as I can how to make this nutso career work for them.

I truly believe there's not much more to this world than the stories we tell. I don't mean to completely uproot you from all you hold dear, but is there any set purpose in life other than the one each of us makes for ourselves?

That purpose is a story we're telling ourselves, where we're the protagonist. That doesn't make it immaterial or unimportant or frivolous. Quite the opposite. It makes story the most important thing in the multiverse.

Everything is made of story. Let's make our stories count.

CHAPTER 2
WHAT ARE THE NINE TYPES?

TWO DIRECTIONS OF MOTIVATION

There are two directions of motivation, whether we're talking about internal or external motivation. Most simply put, these two directions are *toward* or *away*.

When we grab a pot on the stove without realizing that it's hot, we move our hand away. Quickly. (And if you're like me, you curse until you run out of dirty words and have to invent new ones.) When someone puts a big plate of fresh cookies in front of us, we move our hand toward. And both actions are taken without much conscious thought. It's instinctual that you reach for something delicious and that you jerk your hand away from something hot. It's a little thing we like to call survival instinct. Go toward the things like sugar that can sustain you and give you lots of calories so you don't starve to death when food is scarce (at least, that's how we evolved to love sugar so much, even if that particular survival instinct might be upside down at this point). We move away from the things that can harm us, like a hot stove, or a rattlesnake, or the school bully.

None of this will come as a revelation for you, but I mention it to illustrate that there are two driving forces for sentient beings: attraction and repulsion.

These two forces, pushing and pulling, are often referred to as "the stick" and "the carrot." That presumes you're a donkey either driven forward with a stick thwacking your backside or trotting forward out of an internal desire to eat the carrot dangling in front of you. Still pretty simple. Sometimes folks will talk about the "stick-and-carrot approach" as being unproductive, but that's usually when we are discussing external motivators.

It is possible to think of internal motivation as a stick and carrot, too. You have a stick and a carrot that function inside of your brain. The stick is called "fear" and the carrot is called "desire." We move away from our fears; they negatively motivate us. And we move toward our desires; they positively motivate us.

When it comes to the Enneagram, each of the nine types is defined by its specific core fear and core desire. These end up being two sides of the same coin. Together they make up that type's "core motivation."

How is this knowledge of motivation useful to your writing? You need to *move* your characters, to get them to do things that advance the plot and make it interesting to read while also staying true to their character. The word "motivation" is a derivation of the word "motive," which comes from the Latin *motivus*, which means moving. If you want to move the pieces of your story, you must motivate your characters.

How do we make sure that we've done that with consistency in every scene we write? How do we move our heroine to, say, Cairo, Egypt, from Omaha, Nebraska, in a way that makes sense for that character, rather than some way that feels contrived? (I understand that everything we write is technically contrived, since we are contriving it, so what I mean is making sure it doesn't *feel* contrived. We all know the difference, because we've all felt that something was "contrived" while reading someone else's book or watching a movie.)

If you know that your heroine's core fear is, say, being trapped in emotional pain, then you're halfway to figuring out how to get her to Cairo. Insert that core fear to her life in Omaha, and add the promise of rescue from that fear—you guessed it—in Cairo. Threaten with the stick (fear), then dangle the carrot (desire). You know exactly what the donkey will do.

This works for your characters, but it also works for you.

THE ENNEAGRAM

If I were to tell you that there are only nine types of people in this world, you would probably get a little bit annoyed with me, and for good reason. It's not true.

But I have to clarify that anyway because of what we're about to cover in this chapter, which is the nine types of the Enneagram. Yes, I will be encouraging you to figure out which of the nine types is yours, but within each type, there is a spectrum of personality informed by life experience, temperament, talents, and so much more.

No one wants to feel like they've been completely figured out, and that's not what this is about. It's not like you're going to learn about the Enneagram and then suddenly be able to do that psychic crowd work stuff that we all know is probably fake but kind of hope is real. First and foremost, the Enneagram is a tool for *self-discovery*, not any sort of creepy manipulation of others.

And any two people who share a type can still behave quite differently.

When it comes down to it, the Enneagram is about *motivation.* What motivates you to do the things you do? We've already talked about motivation in the introduction, so you might see where I'm going with this. Understanding motivation is an incredibly useful skill for fiction writers, and nonfiction writers, because it teaches you what buttons to press in your characters to make them do what you want them to do in a believable way.

Too many authors get character motivation just plain wrong. You can make your characters do whatever you want (once you learn how), but if their expressed motivation makes little sense or is inconsistent with previous behavior, readers are going to notice, and you're going to get those reviews saying, "This character would never do this thing." Nothing yanks a reader out of a story faster than that.

The biggest and most profound benefit of learning about the Enneagram is that it helps you connect to yourself, and we're only able to connect to others as much as we can connect to ourselves. A sense of disconnection from self is almost always what spurs harmful behavior to ourselves and others. Could the Enneagram solve all the world's problems if each human committed to learning about it? Nah, probably not, but it would certainly put us in a better position to solve them.

Before I get too deep into the weeds, let's take a look at the Enneagram itself and how it breaks down. I love the graphic that's used for the Enneagram. It's sort of perfect. It's got a nice, sacred geometry *feel* to it. And if you're a skeptic of all that like I am, that's fine, too. Just stick with the psychology part and don't go down that other rabbit hole.

In the figure below, you'll see a bunch of arrows pointing from one number to the next. Don't worry about those yet.

Just take in the majesty of the nine types of the Enneagram.

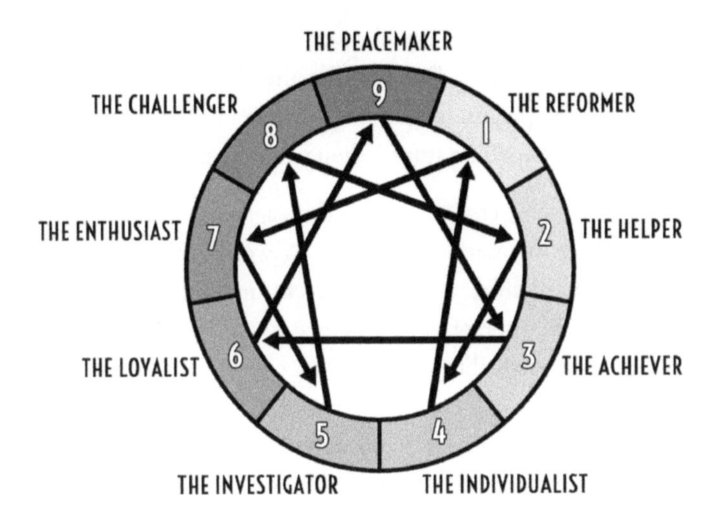

Each type is assigned a number and a descriptive name. You might see a few that resonate with you already, and that's great, but no need to know your type yet.

I use the Riso-Hudson name types for the Enneagram because I think they're the most accurate and show each type in the most positive light. (As an example, some models will call Type 1 "the Perfectionist," which has a seriously negative connotation. As a Type 1 myself, I much prefer the label of "the Reformer.")

I frequently reference the Enneagram in my consulting. Not only do I use it to help authors understand themselves and their career, but I use it to help them understand theme and the characters that they're writing.

The Enneagram is a personality profile. And stories are things *happening to people*. I really hope I don't have to make the case for why understanding people is important to be a strong, effective fiction writer. If you're not clear on that, there are probably better books to be reading. But if you're already sold on the idea that gaining a deeper understanding of human behavior helps you write more compelling stories, then you're in the right place.

Side note: In its most essential form, Enneagram is a framework for the language of emotion. It gives us words for things we hadn't considered before, and that helps us understand how the complex concepts interact and influence us. If you're not huge into the idea of personality profiles, then consider thinking of it simply as a language chart. There's no magic to it, and the more you learn about it, the clearer that becomes. We can't understand the things we don't have the language for, so here is the language of YOU.

ELEMENTS OF THE ENNEAGRAM

Let's start at the simplest level of Enneagram learning by talking about the way it's laid out and a few key terms.

Types: There are nine types within the Enneagram, each defined by a specific core fear and core desire. Together, fear and desire make up motivation. You can think of these as the gas pedal and the brake in your car. Desire makes you hit the gas; fear makes you hit the brake. When I refer to a person's "type," what I'm really referring to is their "dominant type," meaning the type that wins out in the end, the main lens through which a person views the world.

Wings: Since the Enneagram is constructed as a circle, each type has two types flanking it. Either of those types would be a possible "wing" for the dominant type. Not everyone has a wing, and not everyone only has one wing. We may tend toward a specific wing in a specific situation, and we can usually tap into the other one as needed. The motivation of the wings can help support the motivations of the main type. For instance, I'm a Type 1 (Reformer), and around my family I take on a strong Type 9 wing. In virtually every other facet of my life, I take on more of a Type 2 wing. For this reason, I often refer to myself as a 1 wing 2 or simply a "1w2." There's no such thing as a 1w5 or a 3w6. Only numbers on either side of the dominant type can be considered wings. (9 and 1 are considered next to each other, since it's built in a circle.)

Development levels: Within each of the nine types, there are nine levels of development. These nine levels break down into three types of expression of the core motivation: three healthy, three average, and three unhealthy. 3 + 3 + 3.

So: nine types, nine levels of development each. No one stays at a single level of development for long, as things like stress, secure relationships, trauma, exercise, or a bad case of the hangries can move us up and down, making us slightly healthier or unhealthier versions of ourselves. The more you learn about your Enneagram type, and the more you learn the language of this system and unpack your type's unconscious patterns of behavior, the more likely you are to spend a lot of time in the average and healthy levels and rarely dip into the dreaded unhealthy levels.

The reason I use the Enneagram for storytelling and character development, rather than the many other great personality profiles like Myers-Briggs, Cliftonstrengths, or DISC, is that the Enneagram lasers in on the core fears and core desires of each type. To write a good story, you must know your characters' core motivations. You need to know what drives them before you can know what they want and what they need.

But before we even touch your books, we need to know what *your* core motivations are if we're to build you a satisfying career.

At its heart, the Enneagram is a tool for self-knowledge. That's how it was constructed, and that's usually how it is used. We will use it not only in that capacity, but also to the benefit of the selves we must in explore in our story—namely, our protagonists.

BENEFITS OF SELF-KNOWLEDGE

What are the benefits of the self-knowledge that one could gain from the Enneagram?

There are many answers to this, but first let's talk about what happens when we *don't* understand ourselves.

When we go through life unaware of the true needs that motivate our behavior, we aren't in control of our actions and our beliefs. Among other pitfalls of this, such a state of being opens us up to other people manipulating our power and our decision-making skills.

I read a lot of books about cults and emotional abuse, but not because I care to gain that type of control over other people (attempting to manage other people's behaviors is one of my least favorite activities in the world). I enjoy learning about it because I don't want anyone to manipulate *my* actions, beliefs, sense of right and wrong, and, in effect, my brain. You'd be shocked how easy it is to hijack someone else's self-direction, especially someone who is so caught up in unconscious cycles that they don't realize why they do half of the things they do. It's a manipulator's dream to find someone like that, and if there's money to be gained from it, even better.

Obviously, I'm going to the worst-case scenario here, where you mean well but accidentally end up in a cult.

Or am I? Because I think we can all observe cult-like behavior in the people around us. If it happens in others without their knowing, couldn't it also be happening in us? We're all susceptible to cults of personality, but especially when that personality promises us some emotion that we're craving *that we don't realize we're craving* or offers a way of avoiding a fear *that we don't realize is driving us*.

The master manipulator picks up on the core motivations that a person is unaware of after only a few quick exchanges. And once they locate it, they can dangle the most delicious carrot or promise protection from the scariest of sticks.

Our only defense against that is to become aware of what we want on a core level, so that when we identify that something seems to be the answer to that desire, or seems to soothe that fear, we can take a step back and ask ourselves, "Is this going to help me, or is this person offering this to me in the hope that I will give them something they want?"

This level of critical thinking can only come after developing a deep sense of self-knowledge. We develop an alarm system that trips when our deepest desires and fears are activated. That allows us to proceed mindfully and be the ones in control, not the ones easily controlled.

You can develop this system through years of therapy, or you can gain it through learning about something like the Enneagram. As someone who has gone through years of therapy, I'm here to tell you that my self-study on the Enneagram is a hell of a lot cheaper. But doing both is ideal.

Aside from possibly sparing us the humiliation of waking up one day and realizing we are in a destructive cult, the Enneagram and the self-knowledge that we can gain from it acts as an important buffer in all of our actions. People without self-knowledge and presence follow this pattern: something happens and they react to it.

Meanwhile, the goal of self-learning, encouraged by virtually every major religion and spiritual practice, encourages us to work toward the goal of this behavioral pattern: something happens, we consider it objectively using the tools that we possess to make sense of the world and ourselves, and then we respond to it.

Not react, *respond.*

You probably have no trouble thinking of three to three hundred people you know right off the top of your head who are the "react" types rather than those who pause and respond. Being reactive is the natural state in which we emerge from the womb. It takes lots of practice and a little bit of luck in running into the right teachers before we learn to respond, or even learn that we *can* respond rather than merely react. Responding thoughtfully doesn't usually feel as good in the moment as reacting emotionally does, so there's a built-in resistance to it. But sprinkle in a little wisdom, and it's easy to understand the long-term benefits of it.[1]

The Enneagram gives us a blueprint for how a person, given their core fears and desires, can move from that lower state of reacting into a higher consciousness of responding, and in doing so create a stronger and truer connection to their self. The blueprint does not look the same for everyone, because we react to different stimuli more strongly than others depending on those core motivations that drive us, as well as how other factors of our background have shaped us.

Self-knowledge and increased ability to respond thoughtfully will also prove a boon in your writing. Once you understand the mechanics of it, you'll have a much easier time charting your protagonist's arc.

When it comes down to it, almost every story is a tale of our protagonist moving from that state of reacting (passive) into one of responding (active) by gaining the necessary self-knowledge to advance down that path.

Does that sound like oversimplification? I'll grant you that it might be, but not by very much. Think about your favorite story. Does it fit this pattern? Did the protagonist begin the narrative caught up in some unconscious cycles of behavior that, through the course of the plot, they began to gain more awareness about, and in doing so, move from a reactive state to a place where they could *make a decision* and *respond* in such a way that they were able to resolve their conflict?

Don't worry, we'll go into the protagonist's journey more in the chapter on protagonists.

The important thing to note now is that the Enneagram is a tool that can take us from reactive, unaware beings into responsive, self-aware leaders in our life. That's why it's so damn powerful.

Before you can take advantage of the many benefits of the Enneagram, you must figure out which of the nine types you best fit.

FINDING YOUR TYPE

There are many reasons why I suggest every single author, and every single *person*, for that matter, identifies their Enneagram type and learns about it. Not only does it help you in your interpersonal relationships from here on out, but it shows you things about yourself that you didn't know or had never looked at from that angle. There's a fantastic quote from Marilyn Vancil, a well-known Enneagram expert, that describes the system thus: "The Enneagram clarifies the ways in which we are held captive by habitual patterns we are most certainly unaware of."

It's the word "unaware" that draws me to that quote. How much do we do in our life that we are unaware of, that is little more than a pattern of behavior we've never examined? And how often do those patterns of behavior *work in our favor*? In my experience, almost never.

Our patterns of behavior are things that we learned when we were young because, for one reason or another, they were advantageous.

Good for our younger selves, but we're adults now. A lot has changed. The blind obedience that might've kept us alive as a child isn't so cute anymore. Neither is black-and-white thinking or consistently demanding that our needs be met by others.

Your environment and brain have changed significantly since you were a child, so the patterns of behavior you developed back then probably deserve a second look.

My guess is that you'll find you don't need a lot of them anymore. They "no longer serve you," as a therapist would say.

In the context of being an author, this looks like learning bit by bit what we need from our career to feel satisfied rather than letting existing behavioral patterns lead us to a place that doesn't bring us the fulfillment we hoped it would.

Often the unconscious behavior was never *designed* for fulfillment. Rather, it was designed to make us feel safe or worthy or self-sufficient or righteous and is now unsuccessful at making us feel *any* of those things in a true way.

Now we're getting pretty deep, aren't we? I told you this was going to feel a little bit like therapy.

Let's move on to figuring out what your type is. If you already know your Enneagram type, you're a step ahead. If you don't know yours yet, there are some great tests to take out there on the internet, many of them free, and plenty of great resources to read up on the different types and complete a self-assessment (depending on the stress levels of your life when you take the test, your top result might not be precisely accurate, so reading up on your top three or four scores is always recommended)[2].

A test is not necessary, per se, because you can look at brief descriptions of the types and a few will start to stand out to you as "Yes, that's me!" or, similarly, "That doesn't sound anything like me, and I don't think I would like that person very much."

There is a lot to talk about for each of the nine types, but for the purposes of alignment (which is what this book is about, remember?), I'm going to focus primarily on core motivations. Remember, motivation breaks down into two parts, the things we move *toward* and the things we move *away from.*

Here are the core motivations for each of the types:

ENNEAGRAM CORE MOTIVATIONS

Type 1, the Reformer

Desire: to be good | Fear: being bad, corrupt

Type 2, the Helper

Desire: to be loved, needed | Fear: being unloved, unwanted

Type 3, the Achiever

Desire: to be worthy, valuable | Fear: being worthless, valueless

Type 4, the Individualist

Desire: to be uniquely themselves | Fear: being insignificant

Type 5, the Investigator

Desire: to be competent, capable | Fear: being incompetent, incapable

Type 6, the Loyalist

Desire: to be supported, secure | Fear: being unsupported, without guidance

Type 7, the Enthusiast

Desire: to be satisfied | Fear: being trapped in deprivation, pain

Type 8, the Challenger

Desire: to be strong, independent | Fear: being controlled, harmed

Type 9, the Peacemaker

Desire: to be whole, unified | Fear: being separate, cut off

Go ahead and bookmark this page so you can check back, since we'll be discussing these frequently and you might want a reference.

The core motivations alone probably feel like little to go on, so for the sake of helping you with the process of finding your type, I'm going to do something risky and give you a brief and oversimplified rundown of each. Just keep in mind that what I'll be describing is mostly behavior, which is *resultant* of the core motivations. There's a wide variety of ways each type can manifest in thoughts and behaviors, so I'm aiming my arrow at the most common ones I've seen and am by no means hitting the full spectrum. (Lord save me.) Okay, here we go...

Type 1, the Reformer

Morally gray areas are uncomfortable, but thankfully you're an expert sorter of all things into right and wrong. You've been called a perfectionist frequently in your life, but it's not your fault you have high standards for everything. How else would things get done the right way? Sometimes you're so angry at the injustices of the world that you want to scream, but there's not an appropriate time or place for it, so you'll choke it down and work harder on trying to fix what's broken. There are days when your inner critic is so loud that you want to give up, agree with the jerk, and crawl under the covers. But you don't. At least not permanently. You have a vision of a better world, and it's your mission to move yourself and others toward it, whether you enjoy it or not. You spend a lot of your time thinking of the best way to live your life while causing the least amount of harm. Your friends come to you for wisdom and rely on you for your integrity.

Things that push you over the edge:

- Hypocrites
- Lack of integrity
- Your own mistakes and shortfalls

Type 2, the Helper

You don't understand how the world can be so harsh. When those around you need help, you're the first one to offer it. Sometimes even when they don't need help, you're the first one to offer it. After all, what good are you if you're not helping? A refusal of your help can feel like a rejection of you as a person, so you build a life full of people who need you. If someone asks you what *you* need, though, the answer is always "Nothing, I'm good." That is, until you aren't anymore. Then you find yourself looking around and wondering why no one anticipates your needs like you do theirs. You don't want to be bitter, but you can't help it sometimes. They shouldn't have to ask what you need, they should just *know*, like you did with them. You spend much of your life anticipating the needs of others, and your sensitive nature makes you incredibly talented at it. You're frequently called nurturing. Your friends know that you'll always be there when they need a shoulder to cry on and a warm meal.

Things that push you over the edge:

- Inconsiderate people
- Lack of reciprocation
- Rejection of your help

Type 3, the Achiever

Productivity comes naturally to you. You have a gift for anticipating the desires of those around you, especially whom they would like you to be, and you understand that fulfilling those desires is the easiest way to achievement. You've been called charismatic before. You've also been called a chameleon. Sometimes playing the part becomes exhausting, like a never-ending job interview, but when you think about all you have left to accomplish, you don't see another way to the finish line. Whatever you choose to do in life, you earn high marks, awards, and bonuses... otherwise, you don't do it. You have no problem promising to deliver on something before you know how you'll get it done, because you trust in your work ethic and savvy to find a way to at least meet the bare minimum of what's required to please others. Your friends are in awe of what you've accomplished, and when they need help figuring out a path forward, they seek your counsel.

Things that push you over the edge:

- Being called fake
- Going unrecognized for your hard work
- Attacks on your reputation

Type 4, the Individualist

The world is a messy and complicated place, and those who believe they understand it are missing the point. You didn't choose to be on planet Earth, but now that you're here, perhaps you should explore your place in the chaos. You've been called artsy or overemotional for most of your life, but that's just a byproduct of your search for your true self. You feel emotions, especially the darker ones, strongly, and you channel that in your various fantasies. You like things messy because chaos seems to shake out the truths and expose the frauds around you. Order is a coping mechanism for other people, but it's not the true way of the universe. Nothing can truly be understood, not even you. You're usually the oddball of the group, and you prefer friends who don't act like they have it all together. When one of those friends feels down, they trust they can share the dark parts of their life with you without judgment.

Things that push you over the edge:

- Being pressured to conform
- Poor taste
- Forced positivity

Type 5, the Investigator

You wish you had more time on this earth for your research. When you find a topic interesting, you naturally fall headfirst into it and become an expert without thinking twice. You live your life rationally, trying to correct for the occasional emotions you feel that could bias your logical thinking. You're a problem solver, because how else would you use your time? You've been called private or emotionally unavailable more than once and by many people. While you enjoy observing others, the demands of interpersonal relationships can feel like they're draining the life from you, and you need that energy for your learning and research. When you do get started talking about one of your pet topics, though, you can happily go on for hours. Your friends come to you when they need information or an objective opinion from someone who won't gossip about it after.

Things that push you over the edge:

- Intellectual incompetence in positions of power
- Willful ignorance
- Being told your facts are wrong or "just your opinion"

Type 6, the Loyalist

The world is a scary place, and the best way to get through it is by making friends. You often sort people into allies and enemies, and you have a sixth sense for threats. When you find people you trust, you give them your complete loyalty... until they show signs of a possible betrayal, and then they're cut off. You're a responsible person by nature, understanding that adhering to the rules and expectations placed on you is the easiest way to keep a low profile and avoid a target on your back. You've been called anxious more than once in your life, and those people don't know the half of it. You wish everyone could approach life more cooperatively rather than scheming and exercising rugged individualism. Things work better when people work together. But you know that never lasts. Someone always betrays the group, and when they do, you've usually seen it coming. You struggle to trust authority even as you look to authority figures to protect you. Your friends know that you have their back and will be there to wholeheartedly cheer them on.

Things that push you over the edge:

- Perceived betrayals
- Lack of loyalty
- Being told to relax

Type 7, the Enthusiast

There are so many enjoyable experiences in this world, why hold yourself back? The world is full of possibilities, and you're not going to let anyone stop you from pursuing them as you will. The people you spend the most time around are those willing to come along on your adventures, but almost all of them seem to drop off eventually. You've been called scattered or avoidant more than once, and your ability to simply "move on" from an unpleasant situation has left friends with hurt feelings in your wake. What are you supposed to do when your mind goes a mile a minute and there are still exciting places and foods to explore in this one life—sit still? Just because you prefer to focus on the positive doesn't mean nothing ever gets you down. But when it does, you pop right back up quickly. Too much to do to stay low for long. Your friends know you're always up for an adventure, and they reach out to you when they need to get away from their troubles for a little while.

Things that push you over the edge:

- Being stuck in an unpleasant situation
- Detail work
- Chronic worriers

Type 8, the Challenger

There's no place in your life for people who try to hold you back. You know what you want, and you're doing to get it. God help anyone who tries to stop you. Life is a battle that you intend to win, and your weapons are a strong will, honesty, and fearlessness. Whether you mean to or not, you end up in leadership positions, but you can't abide submitting to the authority of someone else, so that suits you just fine. You're not for everyone, and that's okay. You know that plenty of people find you a little scary, but that's their problem, not yours. When you do find your people, you take them on as your responsibility and will defend their interests as you would your own. You're reluctant to show vulnerability, since it's an invitation for someone to hurt you. When unjust power has taken hold somewhere, you're the first to challenge it. Your friends know you have their back in a fight and are put at ease by the fact that you say what you mean and mean what you say.

Things that push you over the edge:

- Weak leadership
- Public shows of emotion
- Backstabbing

Type 9, the Peacemaker

The universe is one complete body, and you wish everyone would stop trying to separate it out into bits and pieces. You don't understand why everyone is always at odds with each other when they're more the same than different. You easily find common ground with yourself and those around you, and when the other person tries to create conflict, you'd much rather acquiesce than engage. You enjoy the comforts of life, maybe a little too much. How else are you supposed to preserve your inner peace but to withdraw occasionally from reality? You say yes to things only to realize once you're committed that you really meant no. You've been accused of being passive-aggressive more than once. You can see situations from every point of view, which makes you a fantastic mediator and terrible at deciding where the next family vacation should be. Your friends come to you when they need calm from the storm or a nonjudgmental friend to listen to their woes.

Things that push you over the edge:

- Being rushed to make a decision
- Closed-mindedness
- Having to pick sides

Did you see one that really resonated with you? Maybe a few? If you read one and felt like you'd just been kicked in the chest, that's probably your type.

It's common to relate to multiple core fears or desires. We are complex beings who will fear all of these things at least a little and desire each of these things at least a small amount, too. If you're a Type 4, Individualist, it doesn't mean that you're not at all concerned when you end up in a situation where someone might harm you (the core fear of the Eight, Challenger). It just means that, if you were in a situation where your choice was to make yourself vulnerable to harm *or* commit to being someone you're not, you'll probably choose the former over the latter. Your core motivation wins out above all others if you have to pick.

That's a trick I suggest for people who are struggling between a few types. Imagine a scenario that pits two likely candidates against each other. Say you're undecided between One and Eight. In a situation where you could *either* do the thing you know to be morally right (Type 1) *or* protect yourself from being harmed by others (Type 8), which would you choose? Which have you chosen in the past?

(Fun fact: if your inner critic is incredibly vocal, you're more likely a One than an Eight.)

There are plenty of great books on the Enneagram that can help you sort through this further and then learn even more about your type. So, if you want to go deep to learn about this, that information is out there, and I've included a list of them in this footnote[3]. But if you just want to figure out what your type is and get on with this alignment thing, I don't really blame you for that either. I'm an incredibly impatient person myself.

Ultimately, this is a tool of self-knowledge, and no one can know you better than you can know you—but settling on your type can often take some work and a coach (like me) to help you ask the right questions.

Only once you know your type can we truly and deeply explore your motivations. And once we understand your personal motivations, then we can drill down in those concentric circles of alignment in the author career.

EXAMINING OUR FEAR

When we look at the career we're trying to create for ourselves, we need to know what we're scared of so that we can accurately assess whether this fear is founded or blown out of proportion. This will go on a case-by-case basis, but the more aware we are of it, the more objective we can be. And when we can't be objective, we have friends with different core fears who can be.

I have a *few* fears, as most people do. We are not limited to one. My fears are mostly ones that I've had my whole life but can't quite shake. Some need to be acknowledged and respected, and others need to be worked through because they make no fucking sense.

It's the nature of fear to puff itself up as big as we allow it to, so the best thing we can do is to take a moment to look at the totality of it and ask ourselves which parts of its bloated form are worth respecting, and which are causing us to miss out on the bounty of life.

For instance...

I have a massive fear of snakes, which is rotten news for me, since I live in Texas. My neighborhood makes the news each year for the mindboggling number of rattlesnakes that turn up on back porches or in garages each summer. I could lie and tell you I'm scared of *only* snakes, but, in fact, my heart rate shoots up when I see *anything* that resembles a snake, be that an extra-large worm, a discarded length of rope in the street, or a *picture* of a snake.

That's objectively ridiculous, right? Images of snakes are not real threats to me. Neither are earthworms. So, if I don't examine this expansive fear, then I'm going to act like a gosh-darned fool rather than an adult with a mortgage. So, once I examine my behavior and objective circumstances, I can say to myself with some certainty, "You don't need to be scared of things that are snakelike but not snakes."

Let's examine the snake fear even more closely. Does it make sense for me to be afraid of *all* snakes? Because, yes, there are a lot of rattlesnakes slithering about, but there are also plenty of harmless snakes in my neighborhood, and more than that, there are harmless-to-me snakes that will eat rattlesnakes and the food that rattlesnakes need to survive and will thereby help manage the horrifying rattlesnake population.

If I fail to examine my fear of snakes closely, I might end up killing (fight) or running from (flight) every snake I see, and that's not good for my reputation *or* the neighborhood *or* the harmless snakes. In letting my fear go unexamined and, let's say, running over harmless snakes with my car, I unwittingly encourage the rattlesnake population, the one thing in this situation that I *should* legitimately give a wide berth.

There is no Enneagram type whose core fear is rattlesnakes, but this is a clear example of how our fears can become bigger than makes any practical sense. Only through examining them, piece by piece, can we parse out which elements are useful to surviving and thriving and which are keeping us from healthy functioning.

My Enneagram type is Type 1, the Reformer. The core fear is not snakes. The core fear is being bad, defective, evil, or corrupt. How does that knowledge help me in my life and career? How does knowing that *my deepest fear* is that I have a stained soul beyond moral redemption help me as a human being live a more rational life?

It goes back to the idea of responding rather than reacting. Once we dissect our fear and learn more about the ways it affects our reactions, we can start to respond with the question "Is this something I need to fear? Or is this triggering that core fear response in me that I've let grow too large?"

Once examining our fear becomes a matter of habit for us, we have a *choice* of how we respond.

Is that really a rattlesnake? Or is that a harmless snake that wants nothing to do with me, and I'm allowing it to frighten me across the street because I didn't take the time to determine whether it's venomous? I'm letting that snake *move* me from my path.

Except, once I take the time to identify the species, I see that it's just an average rat snake, probably looking to eat rats, which I am also not a big fan of, and now that I look at it closely, it's kind of cool. I know I can go on my merry way, and not carry forward the adrenaline rush of believing that I was in danger. Maybe I don't have all these rational thoughts the first time I encounter a rat snake, because this kind of thing takes practice, but eventually I'll get there. Progress, not perfection, as they say.

And for a Type 1 (Reformer) protagonist, the trigger for that core fear (being corrupt, evil, bad) might look like a wrongful accusation, a well-intentioned gesture that's misinterpreted as selfish, or a past mistake being used as proof of weak integrity. These triggers will make a Reformer who has not moved from reaction to responding *freak out*. Maybe even lash out.

If this Reformer happens to be one of the characters you're writing, then you, as the author, can dangle that perceived opportunity for moral redemption exactly where you need your protagonist to go. That promise that if the protagonist just does X, she can fulfill her core desire (in the case of the One, being good and virtuous) while also avoiding that core fear is all you need to manipulate her in a believable way. And that makes you incredibly powerful as a storyteller, all while staying true to your character's core motivations. Once you define a character's Enneagram type, you control the stick, and you control the carrot, and you know how to use them.

And once you understand your core fear, you take that stick away from the world.

AUTONOMY, MASTERY, PURPOSE

You may or may not have heard of the three things that, according to social scientists, create workplace happiness. As a refresher, they are 1) purpose, 2) autonomy, and 3) mastery. As an indie author, you have that autonomy built in. You get to decide what you do, how you do it, and when you do it. I don't know about you, but that's most of the appeal for me. I want to write the story I feel compelled to write, without making major structural concessions that some editor working for some goliath publishing house, who has their own made-up explanation for what is selling, tells me to do.

I don't mean to trash the traditional publishing process, but it's not for me. I *love* my autonomy. And my guess is that you love it, too. You love deciding what time you get up in the morning (assuming you don't have kids or a nine-to-five job making that decision for you), when you write, your preferred editing process, what your cover design will be, and so on and so forth. It's a lot of pressure to oversee everything, but most of us wouldn't feel great handing it off to someone else.

So, we have the autonomy thing covered. Mastery is another matter entirely. We can grow bored if we don't improve our skills. Maybe you've mastered the beats of a bestselling romance novel. It's now encoded into your bones what scene should come next. If you don't find something else to improve about your craft, you're going to lose interest over time, and your mind will wander to other genres, other mediums, or other professions entirely in its pursuit of something new to master. That's not always a bad thing, but it can be a problem if it's not built into your strategy.

The fact that you're reading this book tells me that you're up for the challenge of learning new things, and that when publishing begins to feel too routine, you will probably key in to the fact that you need to step up your game—not necessarily for sales purposes, but to keep that creative relationship with your stories fresh and spicy. You sensed that you needed a new challenge, and you've arrived at one with this book. Go, you!

On to that third requirement for work satisfaction: purpose. This one may be the most important of all three, because it provides some structure to decide *what* to do, not just how to do it. That's why, I'm sorry to say, purpose is the most frequently overlooked element of this satisfaction triplet within the indie author community.

Why are you writing? No, I mean it. Why in the hell are you spending your time this way? By all accounts, you shouldn't be.

There are other things you could do. A bunch of them. Many more profitable ones, too. I demand to know why you're mucking about with this nonsense. You'd better have a damned good reason if you're going to last.

Thankfully, there's plenty of discussion about that "why" in author circles. But here's the problem: a lot of authors pick the wrong "why" for them, and that's where the real problems start.

Once we learn our Enneagram type, however, we can ensure that our purpose is aligned with who we are, rather than who we wish we were or who others wished we would be.

THE RIGHT PURPOSE FOR YOU

Why are we embarking on this crazy profession in what is essentially uncharted territory? Why not do something easier? Why not just write as a hobby? These are all great questions, but the problem is that, more often than not, people are looking to *others* to figure out what is an acceptable purpose for them to adopt.

I'm telling you this right now at the risk of someone coming at me: most industry "gurus," the ones who love to get up on stage in front of a crowd and talk about their success, are Enneagram Threes, the Achievers.

There's nothing wrong with being an Achiever! It's just that not everyone is one, and so people in the diverse audience will see that definition of success on the stage or on a webinar, and they'll say, "Oh look! It's success! I want that good, successful feeling!" And then these non-Three people try to duplicate that particular brand of success by attempting to do all the things the Achiever did.

The result is usually an audience of people who look like they're in pain because they think they have to get up on a stage to be successful, and that might be the last thing they want to do. Or they believe that if public speaking and teaching aren't routes that appeal to them, there's some sort of deficiency that will forever keep success out of reach.

And those are only two of the possible misconceptions that can come from trying to duplicate the lauded success of people who don't share your core motivations.

Side note: Achievers are especially talented at getting things done, because they believe that their quantitative accomplishments are what bring them worth. If you're a Three reading this, you're like "No shit, Claire. What *else* would define a person's worth?" (My dear Three, you are already worthy of all the love you hope to receive, regardless of your accomplishments.)

And if you're American, you might also be confused as to what else, besides external accomplishments, would define a person's worth. That's because the United States has a Type 3 *overlay*, and not always a healthy one at that.

An "overlay" in Enneagram speak is a system of values and beliefs shared by a group that is imposed upon the individuals who make up that group.

So as part of the United States' defining principles, we've baked in the core motivations of the Three. Maybe not into the Constitution, but definitely into our version of capitalism.

Capitalism as it functions in America is an incredibly Type 3 system, so even if you're not a Type 3, if you were raised within this capitalist society, you've internalized some of the beliefs, values, and typical thought patterns of the Three. It's important to recognize that Americans have essentially been raised to believe that accomplishment and productivity equals worth. And this is what makes each of us Americans extra susceptible to those shiny Type 3s on stage. We've been raised to believe that hype.

(Every community, from your city to your church to your immediate family, can have a particular Enneagram overlay that colors your perception of reality, but that's more something for you to think about in the car or the shower or wherever you do your deep thinking and less something I have time to get into here.)

Back to what happens when we see those Threes on stage. What's happening for the non-Threes in the audience is often that they begin to adopt ideas of success that do not fit with their core desire. And that leads to adopting the wrong "why" for their career.

Let me be clear: the Achiever's path not a *wrong* path. It's simply not the only road to success, and if you're not a Type 3, other definitions of success will likely bring more satisfaction and fulfillment for you personally. On the hard days, the thought of accomplishment alone may not sustain you, but perhaps the thought of comforting your readers in their dark times or changing hearts and minds for the better will. That's why it's crucial to find clarity on this topic of purpose.

Not to be "that girl," but your purpose for writing is never *money*. If your purpose was solely to max out your earning potential, you would not be in this profession to start with. Creative purpose and monetary goals are *not* the same thing, as we'll dig into in the next chapter. Your purpose in life, the reason you were born (other than your parents getting it on), was not to earn a made-up currency through toil. We need to think bigger, grander, hell, more *pretentiously*. Our purpose must be grand to sustain us.

I'll harp on that more in the next chapter, but insofar as how the Enneagram helps us find a satisfying purpose, each type is attracted to different pursuits resulting from our varying fears and desires. So, when you're looking for your "why," make sure you don't grab somebody else's "why," thinking it will make you seem virtuous or likable or smart or brave or deep.

You need to build a purpose that works for you, because when you don't, what you end up with is years of experience working toward something you don't care that much about. Not only will that be a major bummer to look back on a few decades from now, but an ill-fitted purpose can only sustain you for a little while before it runs out. And once it does, you'll be right back where you started, asking yourself, "Why?"

Here's the great news, though: the best-fitting purpose for each person can be found through alignment with one's core desires. And in the next chapter, we'll talk about how that translates to each type, and how you can pinpoint a satisfying purpose for your career—not only long term, but every day—through a little added self-knowledge.

HOMEWORK

Find your Enneagram type

1. **Take a test**. If you are willing to pay $12, take the one at www.tests.enneagraminstitute.com. There are also free tests online, but be sure the one you take shows your score for each of the types rather than only telling you what type you scored the highest for. I like the test on Eclectic Energies for this reason, and you can take that one here: https://www.eclecticenergies.com/enneagram/dotest

2. **Read up on your top three or four score.** This is so important, because for many reasons, you might not score highest as your dominant type. Sometimes these self-assessments can get a little disorienting, or you're fixated on how you act in a particular setting (work, family, etc.) and it might not be demonstrative of your life as a whole. So read up and see which description fits you best. If you're torn between a couple, try this: imagine a scenario where you have to choose between avoiding one core fear *or* the other. Which would you choose? That's probably your type.
3. **Learn your type's core motivations**. Knowing what you're moving toward and away from at that deepest level is going to allow you to get the most out of the rest of this book. If you're still vacillating between a few types, then read up on those types online or in one of the books I recommended in the footnotes, and you'll likely find yourself leaning one way or another soon enough.

CHAPTER 3
WHAT ARE MY CREATIVE VALUES?

THE BIG PICTURE

In this chapter, we're starting on the first of the concentric circles of our author career, creative values.

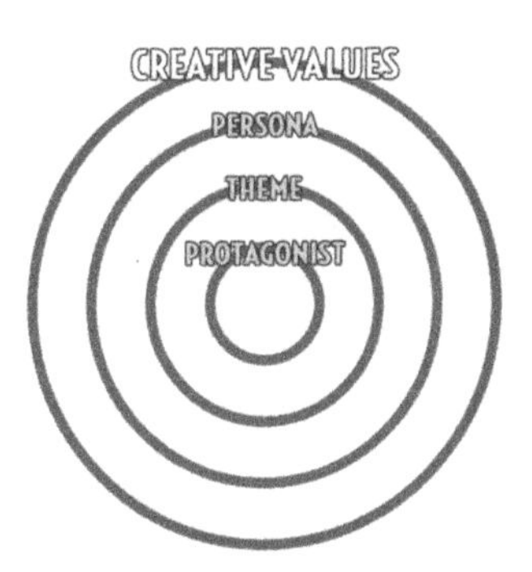

If we're to build an aligned career, we must pay attention to these. Ignoring them is the fastest way to finding ourselves in the last place we want to be, wherever that is. Maybe that's burnout, financial trouble, misery, or lacking respect for ourselves, others, and the industry in which we work. It's not pretty when we lose touch with our creative values, but before we can lose touch with them, we need to discover what they are.

The following sections take a deep dive into those, using the Enneagram as a guide.

WRITING MOTIVATIONS

Being an indie author is a Very Specific Thing. I've never met anyone who slipped on a banana peel and found themselves in this industry. There's also no "My father and his father were both indie authors, so I took over the family business," because indie publishing isn't established enough for that.

This path offered you something you wanted and/or promised to shield you from something you feared deep down, and so you went for it. There's a high likelihood you didn't even know what that motivation was. And maybe you still don't.

Yet.

There are two choices you are making when you decide to become an indie author. They are:

1. I want to write books.
2. I want to publish my books independently.

Let's look at the motivation for the first choice.

Writing books has different payoffs for different people. Why do you want to write? What lofty goal are you working toward? What compels you to sit and write your story when the world is full of delightful distractions that require much less from you?

The answer likely depends on your Enneagram type.

So here are some probable reasons for each type to help you see the scope:

ENNEAGRAM WRITING MOTIVATIONS

Type 1, the Reformer

- To change hearts and minds
- To show people the right way to live
- To create a better world

Type 2, the Helper

- To help people who are struggling
- To build a loving community
- To inspire and uplift

Type 3, the Achiever

- To be recognized for your skills
- To add value to the world
- To be an inspiration to others

Type 4, the Individualist

- To create true beauty
- To express your individuality
- To better understand yourself

Type 5, the Investigator

- To explore life's mysteries
- To build your very own world

- To create puzzles and solve them

Type 6, the Loyalist

- To play in a safe world
- To confront scary things
- To inspire bravery and courage

Type 7, the Enthusiast

- To have adventures and explore
- To keep yourself entertained
- To spread joy to the world

Type 8, the Challenger

- To make your own rules
- To challenge existing norms
- To empower others

Type 9, the Peacemaker

- To find inner peace
- To share your hopeful vision
- To create harmony from conflict

There are more possibilities for each type, but you see how different the reasons can be from one set of core motivations to another. But if you're going to define what you value as a creative entrepreneur, why you put in the long hours, why you get back up again when you fail (for the thousandth time), and why you keep dealing with the inescapable bullshit of this line of work, you have to know what is driving you so you can a) make sure it's sufficient, and b) remind yourself of it when you're frustrated.

Did you notice that none of the reasons listed in the table above mentions money?

While everything seems to be about money, nothing is about money. Not even money is about money. It's all about how having, not having, earning, and spending that resource makes us *feel*. Both fear and desire are *feelings*. We're not as logical as we'd like to believe, unfortunately. But we have this great thing called self-awareness we can develop to take back the reins.

Look at those writing motivations again, this time focusing on the writing purposes that *do not* fall under your type. Can you see how you might find yourself attracted to one of them? Or how you might think, *Oh yeah, that looks good enough, and it'll please my parents/friends/religious group, so I'll make it my purpose.* If you look at it objectively, though, would it be enough to last? Or could you see the motivation quickly running thin in those long hours where it's just you and your computer?

The trap is that you can choose something misaligned with who you are and have it work out *for a while*. But on those hard days, the ones where you're thinking about quitting and playing the cryptocurrency game instead, those misaligned purposes aren't going to cut it. You need to make sure that your purpose is in alignment with your type.

For instance, I think the idea of writing as a means of exploring life's mysteries sounds pretty fun. I could probably write about five books with that express purpose. And then, if I know myself at all, I would sit down at the computer one day and say, "I'm so sick of plumbing life's mysteries. Just give me some fucking answers already!"

That would be my Type 1 coming through. Reformers like me prefer to have answers, solid premises, givens upon which to build our morality and ethics without having to wonder constantly if we've done the wrong thing and harmed people when we meant to help. Realizing you've caused harm when you meant to help is an inciting-incident-worthy realization for a One, and we *don't like it*. Not everything has to be black and white for us (and finding the gray is one of our important challenges to tackle), but we need *something* solid beneath our feet so we can do good and be good, but most importantly, *feel* that we're good. So, yeah, a lot of those purposes won't fly for me, even though I can look at it and think, *I would get a lot of praise if I pursued that,* and the idea of receiving praise is appealing for pretty much everyone.

And that's the point of this as an individualized exercise. Finding your purpose for writing means understanding what will sustain you.

While I can't sustain myself on the great mysteries of life in the long term, I *can* throw my heroines into morally and ethically precarious situations and have them spend the book trying to sort it all out. That definitely gets me going, but, as you're seeing, it won't do it for everyone. And that's fantastic! The various creative needs are what foster a diverse and healthy ecosystem of stories for people of all types.

STAYING ON TRACK

One of the rules of Enneagram is that you're not supposed to type your friends. Or your enemies. But I care a lot less about what I do to my enemies than what I do to my friends. The point is that you're supposed to let people figure out what their type is on their own, because that investigation is part of a crucial self-discovery process that can't be skipped or "hacked."

And yet... I've been guilty of sitting at author conferences, watching the panels give advice, and listening for the keywords, talk styles, and expressed maxims that allow me to make an educated guess on each speaker's type. And then I treat the unlucky friend next to me to lots of "Oh, he's for sure an Investigator," or "Surprise, surprise! Another Achiever saying, 'If I can do it, so can you,'" or "Color me surprised that an Individualist is turning up his nose at writing to market."

This is not to disparage any particular type—all types are wonderful and necessary for a healthy society. I guess the types of those around me to help filter out what is for me and what is not for me (partly a result my Reformer's need to sort the world, but a useful skill for all types). I do it to remind myself that the core motivations that led to that particular brand of success might not be in alignment with the ones upon which I best function. Therefore, this person's path to success is almost guaranteed to not work for me.

The last thing I want is to see more people in this industry lose sight of their own gifts and try to take on core motivations that aren't their own. In other words, I would love to see everyone in this industry happy and emotionally fulfilled by their work.

There are so many ways to be an artist, and one of the most valuable creative skills is being able to say, "I am not doing it that way."

There are plenty of authors whom I admire, whom I think are doing inspiring and impressive things, and my impulse when I witness that is to say, "That. I would like to be that."

There's nothing wrong with striving to become like the kind of people we admire. But we don't always admire people with the same core motivations as us, and our motivations will ultimately determine what weight we assign to certain values. Say you admire someone who is willing to sacrifice personal joy to write twenty-four books a year. Wow, right? That's a lot of books. It's more books than most people write in a lifetime, and this person did it in a year! Impressive, no doubt about that.

But if you're, say, the Type 7: Enthusiast, and your core motivations are to *not* be trapped in pain but to instead pursue satisfaction (this type is sometimes called the Epicurean), then joy is going to be a prized possession, something you strive for in your daily life, and not something you want to sacrifice for money or any other reason. You're not willing to sacrifice joy like they are because you naturally value it more, so if you attempt to reproduce the efforts of that prolific person you admire, you'll quickly find yourself in a state of misalignment and misery. You might not even get *one* book written in a year as a result of being future focused on how much you have left to get done and *Oh my god, I'm going to be stuck in this pain all year, and that's practically forever!* Activate Enthusiast core fear! React by finding a pleasurable distraction!

Meanwhile, if you'd approached it as "I enjoy the escape of writing, so I'm going to go at my own pace and savor every day," you'd probably get at least one, if not more, books written in that year.

That's why it's so crucial to understand your alignment, so you don't end up running yourself into the ground or sacrificing something that you're not willing to forgo long term in the pursuit of achieving what someone else has achieved.

ENVY AND "SHOULD"

If there's one word that can tip you off to misalignment, that is the word "should." If you feel like you *should* be working harder, pause and ask yourself what that even means. More likely than not, you've begun to compare yourself to someone who is a different Enneagram type, motivated by different things. They could also have a vastly different life situation from you, which can play a huge role and ought not be overlooked. The reason they likely have a different life situation from you? Well, outside of what they might've been born into, they've made a series of decisions throughout their life, and those decisions were informed by, you guessed it, fears and desires that are different than your own.

But maybe you see someone who's been in this industry as long as you have, who is about your age, has your same education, has a husband but no kids like you do, and is coming from a similar socioeconomic background. The only difference? They're selling ten times as many books.

Activate comparisonitis!

"Why am I not making as much as they are?" you ask.

That dangerous word might start to creep in: "I *should* be making as much as they are. I *should* be able to write as many books as they do each year. I *should* be the author interviewed on that podcast." These thoughts alone are damaging, but then this little addendum starts to appear if they go unchecked long enough: "I *should* be the author interviewed on that podcast... *instead of them.*" Or "I *should* be making that much money... *and they shouldn't be.*" That's when we see a little thing called "envy" arrive on scene, and nothing is more toxic to an aligned career than that.

Envy is the feeling that someone has something that you by all rights deserve instead. That can be money, sales, connections, fans, opportunities, cars, admiration, degrees, friends, or anything else that seems advantageous.

Let's face it: so much of this industry functions like a slot machine rather than a linear formula. That means that some authors' rise is literally inexplicable—they sat at the right machine at the right time and hit triple sevens. They got lucky and found favor with the zeitgeist, or their Amazon ad ended up on the home screen of a Hollywood producer, or some guy in their elite college fraternity happened to know the right person and made the introduction (so, yes, some of it's luck, some of it's privilege). It's almost impossible to look at someone who's "made it big" and sleuth out exactly where the magic happened.

So often, we see people doing well who "don't deserve it" because—sorry—no one does *or* doesn't. "Deserving" fame, recognition, or money is such a weird idea to begin with. Who gets to be the judge of that? The whole thing is arbitrary. Would you like to be famous and miserable? Of course not. Could you survive being mostly unknown if it meant you were satisfied with your life? For most people, the answer is a hell yes. Satisfaction, contentment, peace, purpose, joy—these are the things we're after.

You want fame? Okay, why? What emotion do you think it'll bring you? Now we're getting somewhere.

Yet envy is a huge problem in this industry and growing more rampant every day. You don't want to be the source of it. But you will be if you don't eliminate "should" from your vocabulary. Some people, when seeing others with the higher social status they crave, will say, "I guess there's something wrong with me." Those people have comparisonitis, and that's terrible in itself.

But other people will say, "I guess there's something wrong with *the world* and the way that it's set up, because that *should* be me." Those are envious types, and they often feel justified in righting the perceived wrong by trying to take down the target of their envy.

I speak from experience when I say if you spot an envious type in this industry (or life), back the hell away slowly. They are the rattlesnake. This is not a rat-snake drill. Unless they pause and do some serious soul searching, envious individuals are more eager to spend their energy destroying you than they are to reevaluate their own goals and strategies and work toward those. (Side note: while rattlesnakes are venomous and ought to be avoided, they're not assholes like people caught in envy. They're just animals doing their thing. Don't come after me for reptile defamation, PETA.)

I can't tell you how many times I've consulted with authors who say, "I should be making so much more money than I am right now." It's a natural impulse to believe that. There are a *ton* of people pitching that to authors, too: "If you just do X, Y, and Z, you'll make the money of your dreams! And if you don't make the money of your dreams, then you didn't do X, Y, and Z correctly!" Like I said before, there's a slot machine element to all this, not to mention more factors in a given person's life than anyone can accurately account for.

But I get it. I don't fault authors who feel like they *should* be making more money. I've felt that way before. I'd venture most people have. It's a trap you don't want to fall into, though. I encourage you to question that idea, and not just because it involves money, but because it also involves the word "should." It's often based on false equivalencies created through misalignment.

Maybe you've written three books, and they are solid books. You took your time writing those three books, workshopping them, revising them, hiring a professional editor, getting the best covers you could afford, and then you release them just like you've been taught. The story is solid and satisfying, the characters are memorable, the plot elements and tropes are to market, the covers look great and are on genre, and the blurb is punchy and appropriate for the ideal readers.

Yet your sales are still less than someone else you know whose stories are not as good (in your opinion), who did not put as much time into cover design, and who clearly didn't hire a proofreader. What the hell? You should be making more money!

There's a lot to unpack here, and there are many reasons why there are no "shoulds" in these situations.

Is this author you're comparing yourself to writing in the same genre? Are they hitting more popular tropes than you? Are they building a stronger email list than you are? Do they have connections to other authors in the genre with existing audiences who promote their work? Do they write stronger chapter hooks? Is their oversimplified storytelling fulfilling a need for the target audience? Are you getting too hung up on perfection, and releasing infrequently? Are you focusing on the wrong elements that are slowing you down without adding much to the story? Where might they be spending their marketing money that you can't see on your end? Is that why they're selling ten times the books you are? Or is it possible they hit triple sevens on the slot machine?

The list goes on, but wisdom dictates that if it "should" be that way, then it *will* be that way. So, if it is *not* that way, then it *must not* be that way. We all have to put on our big-kid pants and deal with that reality. Because in the end, how other people's careers shake out has nothing, and I mean *nothing*, to do with our own life satisfaction *unless we make it so*.

I say all this to you out of love and compassion because I've been there myself. Granted, it was only for a short period of time, because I don't have many proxies to compare my writing career to, especially my feminist satire series. (Please, if you know of another feminist satire series in existence, let me know, because I could use some solid comp authors for marketing. This is my hell, and I chose it with eyes wide open.)

When I first went indie, I tried to ride the erotica train. That sounds kinkier than I meant it to, but you know what I mean. I did what people said was the right thing to do for that genre at the time (2015), and it never worked out for me. And I kept thinking, *I should be making more money than this*.

But of course, nah. We know that's not true now. One of the reasons why I couldn't do it like other erotica authors was that there were certain things within the genre that the big-time authors did that I was not willing to do, due to the particular orientation of my moral compass.

Now, that's not to say I was writing clean erotica, because such a thing doesn't exist. I enjoyed writing the taboo stuff, because I find it fun and morally engaging to stick a toe over that line. I'm talking more about the marketing side of things. There were tactics that I wasn't willing to try.

So, once I gave up on that, I started writing the series that I'd been thinking about for quite some time: the Jessica Christ series. It's a satire about the literal Daughter of God who is born in small-town Texas to a teen mama with a foul mouth and a big heart. You can probably understand that the series itself is fairly comparisonitis proof, because what am I going to compare it to? I had to come to terms with the reality that in choosing this series in this genre I was prioritizing one thing over another—namely, what I *wanted* to write over what I thought would make me the easiest money.

I was never under any illusion that I would get rich and famous right away (or ever) from writing this comedy series. And that realistic approach was crucial for saving me from the idea that I *should* be making more money. Folks in the small following I've created sometimes say things like "This should be a bestseller," and I'll say, "Are you out of your mind? There's literally no reason to believe that." Everyone has at least one aunt or uncle who would gasp and clutch their heart at the series title alone. This is not art for the masses.

As I saw it, the publishing gods had asked me to choose between writing something strictly to market that had a better shot of making me money but didn't necessarily fulfill my comedy cravings or writing this stupid-ass series that would amuse me to no end while allowing me to explore a theme that I cared a lot about: goodness. What does it mean to be good? Where does modern religion fail and where does it get it right? What traits and behaviors are considered good for men in society but disparaged in women? And how does our idea of a patriarchal God perpetuate the suffering of people who do not identify as men?

If you've been paying attention, it's obvious why I was, and still am, drawn to these big questions around this theme. I'm an Enneagram Type 1, the Reformer. I was a hopeless case on this front. I had to explore the idea of goodness somehow, and I wasn't willing to sacrifice what others might (controversial takes, my unique voice, general irreverence) to do it. I didn't want to explore the theme within the confines of romance or science fiction (generally more profitable genres); I wanted to do it my way.

Let me tell you, my way is rarely the profitable way. But someone with different core motivations might've created an approach that allowed them to touch on those same questions (in a less direct or less comical way) while also making two or three times the money I did on that series.

Am I telling you that you must choose between writing what you want to write and writing what can sell? Nope! (Put away the pitchforks, please.)

Besides, you don't actually know what will sell and what won't. Remember there's that slot machine element.

All I'm saying is that you must be clear on what you value creatively and how much of each you're willing to sacrifice, and then make your choices accordingly with clear eyes.

As it turns out, by writing *Jessica Christ* my way and not sacrificing those things I cared about, I found the perfect readership for the series and have made quite a bit of money off the books, as well as turning out some hardcore fans who go and spread the Good Word for me. I almost never market this series now, but word of mouth keeps the sales trickling in, because it's unique and relevant enough for people to want to tell others about it. The same uniqueness that makes it difficult to market against comparable series, makes it stand out, and I've been approached with offers to turn it into a musical and a TV series, each avenue an opportunity for expanding the audience and turning more of a profit. (None of the offers have panned out so far, but that's showbiz, baby!)

We'll talk more about why this approach can be so effective in the chapters on Persona, Theme, and Protagonists. *Hint: a ton of my readers are Reformers or strongly admire Reformers.*

I hope you're starting to see how important it is to understand yourself so that you don't fall into these many traps that come with misalignment. Or maybe you only fall into one or two a year. I don't know anyone who has *never* fallen into one. That would be weird.

We were raised from a young age to value certain things in ourselves and the world around us, and many of us are not naturally suited to excel at those specific things. That's not a problem with us, that's a problem with a misaligned society. You need all nine types of people to keep a society in harmony, and things go awry in specific and predictable ways when we don't value all the types equally.

This means that we generally start out from a place of *misalignment* at a young and tender age unless we have adults in our life who see the great things we have to offer as individuals, even if our society/community/family doesn't value those things equally to others.

Since you're a writer, my guess is that you probably did not have enough of those adults in your life as a kid (only partially joking). As a result, you started from a place of misalignment, and now it's your responsibility and no one else's to repair that. And once you do, *everything* will feel so much easier.

RESISTANCE

If you've ever read the book *The War of Art* by Stephen Pressfield, you're familiar with the concept of creative resistance. You don't need to have read that book to have firsthand experience in the matter, though. If you're a writer, you know about it. Resistance can crop up for a variety of reasons. Maybe you're just tired, or maybe you're intimidated by the scope of what you're attempting to pull off, or maybe you're a perfectionist, or maybe there's a voice in your head saying that you should be doing something else with your time. There are all kinds of mental games that can make our attempt to write feel like a waist-deep journey through a bog. The purpose of this section isn't to address all of them, but I will help you face down one variety in particular.

Since this chapter is all about creative values, let's talk about resistance when you haven't set up those values to flow naturally with your core motivations. This leads to that misalignment I talked about in the last section.

Sometimes resistance is an obstacle to be overcome or conquered or pushed through, but when it comes from misalignment with your creative values, resistance is something to listen to and heed. It's the guardrail at the edge of the mountain pass. If you've ever driven on one of those winding roads along the edge of a cliff, and you've been on the outside lane—the one voted Most Likely to Plummet—you don't *begrudge* the guardrail for being there. If you were to veer, you would run into it, and while that might cause superficial damage to your vehicle, it would stop you from ending up in a gorge.

Guardrails are a blessing when your progress is about to take you off a cliff. That's what resistance from misalignment is: the guardrail that keeps you from plummeting.

If you value quality (however you define that) in your writing, but you have started putting quantitative output on a pedestal, holding that up as the marker for "success," and snubbing the part of you that would much prefer to dive deep into the world you're creating and make it rich, engrossing, and error free, you will eventually hit that guardrail in your attempt to be a relentless word machine.

Here's what it can sound like inside that head of yours when you hit your guardrail:

"This isn't going to work anyway."

"I'm so tired."

"What's the point of this?"

"Is it even worth making money off this when I'd be embarrassed by my friends reading it?"

"You're embarrassing yourself."

"Why is this so hard? This should be easy! I'm not even trying my hardest! It should be easy!"

But the sooner you pin down your creative values—that is, the reasons you were drawn to writing fiction in the first place, why you love telling stories, and what they give you on that deep emotional level—the sooner you'll remove this kind of resistance and write the words you care about. You'll stay in your lane on that mountain road, and you won't even notice the guardrail, that's how sure you will feel in your driving.

MONEY MOTIVATIONS

Before we talk about money, I want to revisit your writing motivations. These are based firmly on your creative values, that is, what you find important about this job in a non-monetary sense. If you knew you couldn't make a buck off writing, you might still do it, and if so, why? That answer is what we're looking for with the writing motivations.

So, before we move on, I encourage you to look over the suggested writing motivations again, with particular focus on the ones listed under your type, to get clear on which one or two resonate with you. It may be that your reason isn't listed there, but there are all kinds of reasons that can be derived from the core motivations of each type.

I ask you to do this first, because as soon as we start talking money, all sense can fly out the window.

Great. Now, allow me to be your Virgil as we descend into the many levels of money motivations...

It's important to remember that money is simply a resource. What that resource does for you is a topic that people write lots of nonfiction books about. But I'm going to give you the simplified Enneagram version to get you *thinking* about how you *feel* about money. Of course, as with everything I talk about, I hope that you'll take these ideas and continue to explore them more deeply on your own.

For now, let's look at what money, specifically having plenty of it, might mean to you, depending on your type. People are complex, so within each individual lives healthy and unhealthy ideas about money. But because we know that people pretty much *feel* their way through life—that is, we let our emotions lead the way, spurred on by our core motivations—you'll see that these ideas about money below are feelings based. For each type, I've listed one healthy attitude and one destructive attitude. Shouldn't be hard to figure out which is which.

ENNEAGRAM MONEY MOTIVATIONS

Type 1, the Reformer

- Freedom from sacrificing morals
- Validation of moral superiority

Type 2, the Helper

- The ability to freely help others
- Leverage for being needed by others

Type 3, the Achiever

- Freedom to be authentic
- Validation of value

Type 4, the Individualist

- Freedom to uniquely create
- Confirmation of selling out

Type 5, the Investigator

- Freedom to learn
- Confirmation of intellectual superiority

Type 6, the Loyalist

- Sense of security
- Leverage to keep others around

Type 7, the Enthusiast

- Freedom through options
- Unwanted responsibility

Type 8, the Challenger

- A means for empowerment
- A means for power over others

Type 9, the Peacemaker

- Protection of inner peace
- A substitute for necessary action

Do any of these sound familiar? Maybe a little too familiar? These are by no means all the attitudes possible, but they hit on some deep issues. And when you're in a career that requires you make money off your art, you need to be *crystal clear* what you want both your money and your art to do for you. Because when those two ideas are foggy or, God forbid, conflicting, the amount of energy wasted spinning your wheels, changing directions, or self-sabotaging can be extraordinary. Enough to burn your career to the ground.

To make sure we're clear here, it is the second motivation under each type that is the unhealthy attitude about money. And you might look at it and think, *I would never believe that,* but I beg of you, knock it off. We've all fallen into these traps associated with our type. It's inevitable. In the moment, it's likely that we don't realize we feel the way we do—attitudes are often subconscious until we take time, like we're doing now, to put words to them—but when we're hungry, hormonal, hurting, or simply having a bit of an afternoon cortisol dip, these beliefs easily creep in to color our attitudes and steer our behavior.

This doesn't mean you or I always believe that having money makes us morally or intellectually or creatively superior *all* the time, but when something triggers our core fears, we can jump there in a heartbeat. For that reason, we must pay special attention to it.

Because this part is so crucial to get right before we move on to the other sections and chapters of this book, I'll go more in depth into each type's possible money traps, that is, the unhealthy money motivations. Feel free to skip to yours if you want to get on with it, or read each of them to add a little color to your characters of various types. As is true with all the Enneagram information in this book, what applies to you and your friends can apply equally to your characters.

Type 1, the Reformer

Unhealthy money motivation: validation of moral superiority.

I went to school in Texas with a handful of preachers' kids from megachurches, so this attitude is not unfamiliar to me. It can take the form of what's often called the "prosperity gospel."

Well-adjusted human beings know that someone's wealth is not necessarily an indicator of their goodness or holiness. However, some wealthy but unhealthy folks would love to believe this. It's the idea that wealth equals blessings. If you're an American, you've heard this plenty of times. Maybe you've even implied it yourself by labeling a sudden material gain as a "blessing" without examining what it meant; namely, that those *without* are less blessed by God. That's probably an uglier thing than you meant to imply, I know. But it comes from this negative Type 1 money attitude and that need to feel like a good person at your core.

But think about this: money is just a resource. Do you think the Most Moral Person in the World (whoever that is) is likely to take more resources from others than they give or give more resources to others than they take? Or maybe it's equal. Or maybe it's irrelevant to their goodness. Either way, seeing someone hoard resources (money) doesn't persuade me that they're the role model I necessarily want to put on a pedestal. Can we dispel that unhealthy belief, now that we've held it up to the light?

The idea that money should flow to the purest of the bunch is the unhealthy Type 1 money attitude at its extreme. Your subconscious beliefs might not have been this extreme, but even lesser versions will erode over time and complicate the big decisions you must make for your writing business. For example, will you be more or less willing to invest money back into your business if every dollar you spend feels like a little part of your soul goes with it? What if the investment doesn't pan out? Will you become a corrupt piece of trash?

The answer is no. You'll be the same person, but with a little less cash and new, hard-earned wisdom. That's a pretty good outcome, all in all.

So please, Type 1s, check in with yourself. Are you attaching righteousness to wealth? Or are you using your money as a tool to advance a cause you care about or as insurance against having to go against your values?

Type 2, the Helper

Unhealthy money motivation: leverage for being needed by others.

Have you ever had someone bring you a gift, and your judgment tells you not to take it? Maybe it seems strange that *that* person would be giving you a gift at all? Or maybe you question their motive for giving it? That cautious voice inside you is aware of a little concept called reciprocation. It's a basic element of human society. If someone gives you something, you should really consider returning the favor. We're conditioned to know this is how things generally work. Give and take, and in as equal a measure as possible. This builds trust and stability in a relationship, and we need relationships to survive.

So, what happens when someone gifts you something of great value that you didn't ask for? What happens when you have neither the means nor, perhaps, the desire to return the gesture? It leaves you uneasy, right? You feel indebted, obligated, and in a power-down position, even if you never asked for the gift. That expectation of reciprocation lingers, and if you never fulfill the obligation, you're setting yourself up for being branded a "taker" or a "mooch" later on. Or maybe you're a nicer person than I am, and you spend beyond your means or go out of your way to give a gift back that leaves you even-steven so you can move on with your life, guilt free.

No matter what happens *after* that first unnecessary or inappropriate gift, the act itself has left you in a bind. Did the gift giver mean to do that to you? Who knows? But it still sucks.

Only if you've built strong trust with that giver will you believe it if they say, "I don't need anything from you in return. I thought this would bring you joy, so I would like for you to have it. No reciprocation necessary, because seeing you happy is all I wanted out of this."

This is all to say that it's rare that someone gives us something—money, gifts, help—and we don't feel obligated to give anything in return or expect them to hold it over our heads until we reciprocate.

This is a trap that an average or unhealthy Type 2 will often set for others without even realizing it. Twos are by nature incredibly sweet people, and they *do* genuinely get satisfaction out of showing that sweetness to others. But their core fear is not being wanted or worthy of love, so when this fear takes over, they can fall into patterns of giving at inappropriate times or to inappropriate people. Some Helpers will even give so much that others learn to expect it and become dependent on it, turning the Two into their personal Giving Tree.

It is admittedly a thin line between a healthy use of money to help others and an unhealthy use of it that enables or creates forced reciprocation. A healthy Two will have no problem donating money to causes *anonymously*, because they're following their desire to help rather than their need to ingratiate themselves to others.

Meanwhile, an unhealthy Two might want a building named after her (though she'd never ask it; she'd just expect others to be as talented at reading her needs as she is of theirs so that they magically know she wants a building named after her).

On a much smaller spending scale, a healthy Type 2 might treat his friends to lunch because he loves them, while an unhealthy Two treats his friends to lunch because then maybe they'll feel obligated to invite him to their next party.

In your writing, healthy Two spending might look like buying books of other authors in your genre to read, and then sending them emails praising their work (if you really mean it). Or it could even look like investing in giveaways for your readers or hiring on a novice author as your virtual assistant and apprentice.

So please, Type 2s, check in with yourself. Are you using your money to create codependency or an obligation of reciprocation, or are you using it in a way where the spending itself is reward enough?

Type 3, the Achiever

Unhealthy money motivation: evidence of value.

This view of money is not only unhealthy because it can make the Three miserable, but because it can also make them incredibly hard to be around. The world becomes quite sinister when you allow yourself to believe that people with money have more inherent value than those without. Most of us know, on a spiritual level, that this is not the case.

The biggest trap for a Type 3 is in defining success as "having money," but not necessarily a *specific amount of money*. What are we talking here? Enough to pay the bills? Six figures? Enough to buy a second house in cash? A billion dollars?

The subconscious answer (almost never examined in the light of day) is that the Three has developed a relationship between money and worth that goes like this: more money = more worth. And that's one hell of a slippery slope. Unless you're Jeff Bezos or Elon Musk or whoever is the richest modern robber baron at the time you're reading this, by this flawed logic there will always be someone with more worth than you. And by that logic, you are lacking an amount of the total worth possible for a human being. You are lacking worth.

Rather than pressing pause on this cinema of neurosis and learning to find *innate* worth in themselves, average or unhealthy Threes will usually keep their eyes out for ways to make more money. It's an effective distraction from doing the painful inner work, for sure.

In extreme cases, Threes end up *nobody's* favorite, because they will mistreat or disrespect people who have chosen fulfillment over wealth chasing. Of course, it's all a ruse, and an attempt to cover up their own feelings of inadequacy and unworthiness that come from not having more money than [insert richest person].

A healthy Achiever will establish her purpose and her goals first then work toward earning enough to meet them. And when she meets them, she will *not* immediately move the goalposts, but will take time to celebrate the value she has created in the world. These goals might include mentoring other authors and helping them reach their goals, or even earning enough to take a full month off work in the summer to spend time with her family.

So please, Type 3s, check in with yourself. Are you spending your money to create worth through outward status? Or are you using your money to help bring your talents to the world?

Type 4, the Individualist

Unhealthy money motivation: confirmation of selling out.

Type 4s are stuck in this tug of war between wanting desperately to be understood, and a fear of anyone understanding them. In childhood, they likely felt like the outsider in all things and struggled from a chronic but unnamable longing. It gets tiring feeling so misunderstood, but at least then they feel unique.

This can translate to strange subconscious attitudes about money. The need to be understood drives Fours to write stories with the hope of making emotional contact with others like them, but if they achieve this goal, it can feel like selling out. Because surely no one can connect to their outcast soul in any true sense, so they must have put forth something inauthentic if what they created holds anything resembling mass appeal.

You see why this is a horrible catch-22 for Fours. The result for an average or unhealthy Four will often be self-sabotage. Maybe they stop writing. Maybe they go out of their way to make their stories even more incomprehensible.

Self-sabotage is not a healthy state of living, so the money work of the Individualist is to knock it off with the false equivalence of "royalties = selling out."

I hate you tell you this if you're an Individualist, but one out of every nine people are just like you with that insatiable longing, fantasies that cause reality to constantly disappoint, and the general feeling of being an alien on your own home planet. If you sold a book to roughly one-ninth of all the English-language readers (solely Type 4s), you could make a shit-ton of money without "selling out" by appealing to any of those other eight types.

A healthy Type 4 author can see earnings from their work as a sign that their attempt to connect with the struggling masses is working. They also understand that if they do *not* earn enough to support themselves (assuming they want to be a full-time writer), then they will have to become dependent on others to pay their bills, and that's not ideal for someone who wants to have full say in what they create. More times than not, money dictates artistic freedom, not the degree of selling out.

So please, Type 4s, check in with yourself. Are you sabotaging yourself financially to preserve your identity as unique and misunderstood? Or are you viewing each sale as one more reader whose found your books and might feel a little less like an outcast because of it?

Type 5, the Investigator

Unhealthy money motivation: confirmation of intellectual superiority.

Type 5s are obsessed with the idea of possessing the knowledge they need to be self-sufficient. So, how does money play into that? If they're average or unhealthy, money can function as confirmation that their knowledge is superior to that of others, or that they themselves are intellectually superior. Plenty of folks like to believe we exist in a meritocracy, that the smartest and most competent rise to the top. If this is you, allow me to disabuse you of that belief: think of all the bosses you've ever had. Were all of them smarter than you? More qualified for the job? Case closed.

Because average and unhealthy Type 5s are so head-based and out of touch with their heart and gut, it would be a real shame if they *didn't* believe in their own mental abilities. That's what they value the most starting out.

This desire for self-sufficiency can lead to an impulse to hoard resources, and as we know, money is a resource. If a Five does not have the money they need to be completely self-sufficient, they may equate that with a deficiency of intelligence, and that *hurts*. When that's what you've put on a pedestal at the cost of all else and you don't feel like you have it? Yikes! That's villain origin story material, folks.

On the flip side, if Fives have enough money to be self-sufficient and stockpile a little on the side, they're likely to consider themselves smarter than everyone else around them, and that is a fast way to make sure that there is no one else around you.

A healthy Five writer might calculate how much money they need for their living and publishing expenses, including those required to continue their intellectual pursuits (research, tuition, etc.), and work toward that. They understand that money supports *learning* but doesn't equate to *knowing*, and because of that, they appreciate every dollar for the treasures it can unlock for their curiosity.

So please, Type 5s, check in with yourself. Are you equating money with your intellectual abilities? Or are you using your money to encourage and foster intellectual growth that you can share with the world?

Type 6, the Loyalist

Unhealthy money motivation: leverage to keep others around.

The Six is extremely security focused, which makes them great at risk assessment, but not so great at relaxing and trusting that the relationships they've built will last. As a result, the Six's relationship with money can be fraught. Loyalists embody a contradiction; they can be phobic or counterphobic. For average or unhealthy Sixes, this means they will react to their core fear with a strong fight (attacking the thing that scares them, sometimes to the point of recklessness) or flight (retreating from the fear—usually to a quiet place where they can worry about it incessantly) response.

You can imagine how these two reactions manifest financially. Either way, the Six will often view money, and the way they spend or don't spend it, as a means to build security. This can look like overspending on "just in case" objects (think canned food, guns, bunkers) or simply stockpiling cash rather than letting it flow toward the necessary *investments* we must make in our writing career. In the social realm it can look similar to the Two in that the money might be used as a way to ensure others stay close. But whereas the Twos can spend to ingratiate themselves, the Sixes spend to strengthen their connection to more assertive and authoritative types.

Loyalists can also become a bit miserly about money, opting to save as much as possible, and missing out on certain life experiences because of it. They're so future focused that they forget to live in the present, and nowhere is that more obvious than through unhealthy money motivations.

A healthy Six writer will work toward finding a balance between saving money in the event of a minor emergency or a poor sales month and investing back into their business to promote healthy growth. They may even stay in their nine-to-five longer than other types might out of respect to their need for security while they build a more robust author business.

So please, Type 6s, check in with yourself. Are you relying on money to build an impenetrable fortress around you and your loved ones? Or are you allowing the money to flow in and out of your account in a healthy way that allows everyone to thrive?

Type 7, the Enthusiast

Unhealthy money motivation: unwanted responsibility.

Type 7s like to keep their options open, should an unpleasant situation arise. Unlike Sixes, they don't tend toward worst-case-scenario thinking, but they can be quick to take off or deflect when things get uncomfortable. Many of the Sevens I know have a knack for spending money just as fast, if not faster, than they make it. They don't necessarily waste money on things; they like to treat their friends and go on vacations without feeling that uncomfortable anxiety that comes with questioning whether they have the money to spend on something in that moment. Of course, unless you're a billionaire, you'll probably have to ask yourself, "Do I have the money for this lavish thing?" for the rest of your life. Sevens would rather make it a problem for their future selves to worry about, though.

Delayed gratification can be physically and psychologically painful for everybody, and for the type that is motivated by avoiding pain and deprivation, "delayed gratification" can feel like a nightmare. The good news is that Sevens know how to hustle and find the funds when they need to. The bad news is that they can become stuck in a cycle of working their asses off the last week of each month to make rent.

In the author sphere, this struggle with delayed gratification and wanting to have it all can look like buying pretty covers before knowing anything about the book they plan to write. Or buying courses that they don't necessarily need but could one day prove to be an enjoyable distraction from getting their actual work done. There are two main reasons Enthusiasts end up overspending: they want to experience *all the things*, and/or they view money and the financial tracking that goes along with it as a responsibility that could tie them down or commit them to something unpleasant. This mindset of money as an unwanted responsibility is a big hurdle that the Seven needs to confront before they'll be able to hold on to their money for any period of time.

Healthy Seven authors understand the difference between temporary pleasure (quick fixes) and deep enjoyment (long-term satisfaction). Once they home in on what parts of their career and life bring them the most enjoyment, they can build a career that is extremely fun and allows them the freedom they desire. This could look like using their money to pay a virtual assistant so they have more time to practice their cooking. Or it could look like investing the majority of their time and money in the short term on building a massive and engaged email list so they have more time and money in the long term to travel the world as they write without having to constantly manage ads and promos.

So please, Type 7s, check in with yourself. Are you using your money to distract you from the painful points of your life? Or are you using it as a tool for long-term fulfillment for yourself and others?

Type 8, the Challenger

Unhealthy money motivation: A means for power over others.

Because Type 8's core fear is being controlled or harmed, is it any surprise that when they get a little bit of money, their unhealthy impulse is to use it for control over other people? If you control someone else first, they can't control you. A strong offense is a strong defense. It ain't rocket science. Mostly because it's flawed logic. A need to control others controls you in the end.

When you meet an average or unhealthy Eight on a serious quest for money, watch out, because they're viewing money as power, plain and simple. And if they're at an unhealthy level of their type, that is going to mean power *over*, rather than power with, power to, or empowerment. What will they do with that power? Whatever the hell they want. That's the point.

Challengers have a deep, visceral reaction to vulnerability. Each type has a similarly blinding reaction to one thing or another, but for the Eight, this is it. And they're not entirely wrong about money equaling power, are they? We all see how this place called Earth runs.

It's not exactly a perfect system, is it? (There's my Reformer coming through.) The quest for power over others never ends well, and there will always be someone richer than you and therefore able to harm you if they want. So, if you can't win the game, maybe stop playing it.

Instead, I challenge the Challengers to view money in a more altruistic sense. You hate vulnerability, right? You've probably seen your fair share of people (including yourself) abused and harmed without a way to protect themselves. Why not use your resources to help protect them? In writing, this could look like investing in stories of *empowerment* that inspire people to band together to take on those abusing the power. Or it could look like helping other authors along. A healthy Eight attracts followers with their natural leadership energy, and they don't take that responsibility lightly.

So please, Type 8s, check in with yourself. Are you viewing money as a means to gain *power over* others? Or are you viewing it as the breaker of chains that it can be and using it to help *empower* yourself and others?

Type 9, The Peacemaker

Unhealthy money motivation: a substitute for necessary action.

While Type 9s have a natural gift for defusing tense situations, if they had all the money they needed, many would be perfectly happy to bow out and go find their own peace and solitude away from all conflict. Of course, that's a pipe dream, because there's nowhere without conflict. The Nines can't escape it, no matter how much money they have. But boy will they try. Unfortunately, claiming that everything is fine when it clearly is not doesn't qualify as being peaceful; it's called dissociation from reality. Almost always, conflict *is* required to restore the peace, but Peacemakers would be happier throwing money at the problem, if possible. When average or unhealthy Nines do get money, one temptation is to use it for things that will help them check out from the conflicts of the outer world: books, video games, alcohol, weed, cabins in the woods, and so on. But eventually they will need to act in their life, and no amount of money will do that for them. It will only put it off until the situation is more critical and urgent.

This conflict avoidance comes from the Nine's fear of being separated or cut off from the wholeness of humanity. They don't want to feel like a spare part, and when you engage in conflict, sometimes the result is severing of connection with the parties involved.

So many Peacemakers flock to writing because their stories are somewhere they can show up completely without fear of the conflicts in their story world spilling out into their life. It's a place where Nines can reconnect with the parts of themselves that have merged with others or deactivated in an attempt to keep the peace.

Healthy Nine authors might view their investment in their business as a commitment to exploring the parts of themselves (through writing) that they have hidden away to avoid interpersonal conflicts. They use their money to support the brave and necessary action they must take to bring forth all the parts of themselves that deserve to be revealed and to build a diverse and harmonious community around their stories.

So please, Type 9s, check in with yourself. Are you throwing your money around as means to avoid conflict and insulate? Or are you allowing your money to support you in bringing all of yourself to the world?

THE MONEY LANDSCAPE OF INDIE PUBLISHING

Let's take a closer look at how the creative values and our ideas about money might intersect and either complement or clash with each other.

A growing problem I see is just how much talk there is about money in this industry. Not that money is bad, but because 90-99% of people are functioning with these unconscious and often unhealthy money attitudes, the discussions go off the rails quick and become a vat of neuroses. Seriously, it gets weird.

Go into any large Facebook group and find the first post where someone mentions their earnings. Then bust out the popcorn, a cheat sheet of Enneagram motivations, and let the fun begin as you go through the comment section. Not that I've ever done that, because you're not supposed to type others. But... Yeah, I've done it. Guilty as charged. "Six... Eight... Four... Five? No, One." It's actually amazing how money will make those core fears *pop* off the screen.

I don't say any of this to be disparaging. We are all on our own journey toward Enlightenment and blah, blah, blah. I just mean these public money discussions, whether online or during a panel onstage, are rarely a good look for the folks involved.

But boy, can they be tempting to join if you're making more money than everyone else! Remember what we talked about regarding the envy problems in this industry, though? It might feel good to enter the octagon with a whopping sales figure, but that will get a target on your back so fast it'll make your head spin.

The success stories are broadcast everywhere, regardless. If you don't think too hard about it, you might believe this industry is a gold mine ripe for the digging, like a California 1849 kind of situation. And to some extent, that *was* the case years ago. But nowadays, it's more like California 1855-56. Some people got in early and made a killing, and now they use that money to make even more money (often off the backs of the latecomers who think they'll strike it rich by association). But the easy pickings are much scarcer now. And if you want to earn a living, you can't keep digging in dry land, hoping to strike the motherlode. You must develop your skills.

To take this gold rush metaphor a step further, as the land dries up, people are getting more and more willing to kill each other over a promising spot. Oh yeah, it's getting a little nastier out there. That's a natural consequence of inflated expectations. People get frustrated and fall into that trap of "I *should* be making more money." Then, rather than pausing to adjust their expectations or their strategy, they proceed to lash out at others.

Some of the worst offenders I've encountered are those who struck gold early on. It earned them the high status and large sums of easy money that they became addicted to and came to expect. But as the publishing landscape changed over the years, what worked before stopped being as effective, and they were left with the choice of either accepting that it was mostly lucky timing and not 100% their greatness and superiority that got them where they were (the existentially painful option) or committing their energy trying to keep others down in the hopes of staying on top (less existentially painful, but a real dick move).

We get to opt out of all that mess, though, because we're building fulfilling and sustainable careers for the long haul, not trying to get rich quick.

And to do that, we need to let go of the hope of getting rich quick.

Listen to me here: it's not going to happen. It's not a pathway for you. You can have a manifesting mindset or practice the law of attraction or whatever the hell gets you through the day, but *expecting* your first or even your fiftieth book to magically launch you into the stratosphere and make all your wildest dreams come true is not a strategy. Start expecting this to be a process with ups and downs, victories and losses. One that requires you to align yourself and *work* for it. There are no more motherlodes to tap.

Thankfully, writing is the kind of work that can bring you enjoyment and fulfillment if you make that your priority, but it's going to require all your mental and emotional muscles at various points. You'll need time to rest, and you can take it, because it's not a sprint. You'll work hard, rest, renew, fall in and out of love with your stories, struggle, surge forward, fall back. There is no overnight success to be had. Let that go.

But wait! The success stories are still out there! You still hear about people publishing three books and earning five figures only two months in!

Well, duh. The lottery has a winner, too, but if you make your future happiness contingent upon winning the Mega Millions, there's only a 1 in 302,575,350 chance it'll pan out. (Yes, those are the exact odds.) There's a difference between having faith that things will work out for the best and feeling certain you'll be the one to win the Powerball.

So, yes, every now and then someone will come along and find gold in them there hills. And it can make the rest of us kind of lose our minds. We abandon our well-thought-out strategies and core values to try to rush over to get a piece of it. And guess what happens? Usually, we don't get a piece. And then we return to our old plan, having lost both momentum and time.

That's why it's crucial that we know why we're doing this, what our creative values actually are, because those piddly little gold rushes do pop up every now and again. You must anchor yourself to what brings *you* fulfillment, so you don't keep chasing the so-called "easy money." If you want to be a trend prospector and jump around like that from sub-sub-subgenre to sub-sub-subgenre, fine. It was great talking with you and you can go ahead and shut this book now.

Maybe you make some money writing to trend. But when that trend dies, the books you hurriedly wrote (possibly without understanding the mechanics of what makes that genre tick) could die with it, and you'll be stuck with a bunch of limp and lifeless assets. That's the life of the prospector author.

Many call this "being on the hamster wheel," except hamsters can stop and start as they wish. For authors, the prospector life is more like "Hotel California," where you can check in but never check out.

Unless...

Unless you structure your writing around clear creative and financial aims that resonate with you so deeply that the next time a hot trend comes along and promises indie riches, you can simply look at the genre-come-lately and say, "I'm happy for those authors, if it makes them happy," and then let it pass, knowing you're working toward something more important to your life.

THREE QUESTIONS YOU MUST ANSWER

We've gone deep in this chapter, talking about things both abstract and Big Picture. Hopefully by now we're on the same page about the importance of examining your relationship with your writing and the money you make from it.

I want to provide you with distilled questions that you should ponder now, then again tomorrow, then again in a year, then once again in ten years. While your core motivations stay the same for your entire life, your focus evolves, so answering these three big questions is a process and a practice, not a finish line.

Here are three questions I hope every author who reads this book will consider fully before doing anything else.

Question 1: What do I want my writing to do for me creatively, intellectually, emotionally, spiritually? (Pick the word that makes sense for you.)

Here are some examples of what a person might want their writing to do for them on that deeper level:

"I want my writing to help me tussle with morally complex concepts."

"I want my writing to be a place where I feel safe to be myself."

"I want my writing to be an exciting place to escape to each day."

"I want my writing to empower me in my daily life."

And yes, your answer to this question is very likely going to relate back to your Enneagram type, so if you're stumped, read up on those core motivations.

For example, tussling with morally complex concepts is something a Type 1 will likely enjoy. Why? A story is a safe place to play around with moral and ethical concepts. A Reformer can do so without worrying about whether they themselves are a bad person. In effect, their writing becomes roleplaying forms of morality without negative consequences if they get it wrong. It's a place where everyone can be a little right and a little wrong, but still be sympathetic. This is the lesson that the One needs to learn, that you can and will get it wrong and that doesn't make you irredeemable. Developing that empathy for others (the characters) also unlocks self-compassion that Ones struggle with.

The desire for your writing to be an exciting place for you to escape to has strong Type 7 vibes. Enthusiasts hate being trapped in pain, and, as we all know, life is pain, and anyone who says differently is selling something[1]. Okay, so that's not entirely true (though many Fours may believe it), but the point is that pain exists and there's no getting around it in the long run. Sevens will try, though. Enthusiasts tend toward escapist literature, and that's great! Everyone, regardless of type, deserves the occasional escape, because reality can be brutal. Sometimes our problems are too big, the solution too far off, and if we're to keep going, we need rest. Sevens are absolutely the friends you want around when you need a break and a cheering up. It makes sense that they could create their own escape and excitement through their story worlds. So, if this is you, don't fret, embrace!

. . .

Question 2: What do I want my writing to do for other people creatively, intellectually, emotionally, spiritually?

This one is so important because communication requires a sender *and* a receiver. If you're writing just for yourself, you're journaling. Do you want to be a professional journaler? Probably not. So, the effect you wish to have on your readers is equally as important for creative and professional decision making.

Here are some examples of what an author might want their writing to do for others, and see if you can guess what Enneagram type each might appeal most strongly to:

"I want my writing to help my readers understand their place in the universe."

"I want my writing to make my readers feel seen."

"I want my writing to inspire others to chase their dreams."

"I want my writing to challenge and confront my readers' dearest beliefs about the world."

Once you know what you want your writing to do for your readers, that knowledge becomes the Rosetta Stone to building your persona, themes, and protagonist. And when your offering is crystal clear like that, you'll attract the right readers and repel the wrong ones much faster. You also clear the way for more word of mouth, because you're delivering a consistent experience, and readers will be able to articulate that much more succinctly to their friends who would also enjoy it.

Question 3: What do I want my money to do for me?

Only after you know what you want your writing to do for you and your audience on those deeper levels should you consider what you want your *money* to do for you.

Again, I'm going to direct you right back to those core motivations of the Enneagram. If you're satisfying them through your creative process (emotional, spiritual, creative, intellectual), your reliance upon money to be instant gratification for your desire and an easy distraction from your fear will be much less intense and overwhelming.

I'm not saying that if you find creative fulfillment you suddenly won't need to pay your bills. Unfortunately, you'll still need money for these basic things. But what might also happen is that you realize you can downsize your life to free up more money for the things that matter to you. Or maybe you'll finally drop your deadweight partner with expensive tastes (this is by no means relationship advice, but I've seen it happen). How much of your money habits revolved around trying to self-soothe with *things*?

Things cost money, and they rarely leave you feeling fulfilled. We all know this, even if we work hard to forget it.

So, let's say you're a Type 3, the Achiever. You're afraid of being unworthy of love, so you measure your value by your output, awards, and accomplishments. This is pretty typical. The path for you to walk leads to the realization that you are innately worthy of love just by existing. But we don't have to reach the embodiment of that understanding just yet to start making enlightened decisions. We simply need to learn the path of our Enneagram type and point our compass in that direction.

Threes get a great deal of satisfaction out of being influential and inspirational. They spend their time at work and afterward mentoring because it reminds them that they've accomplished things others wish to accomplish, and it allows them to use their talents, of which they usually have many. This is great! Our Three probably feels emotionally fulfilled on a regular basis.

But imagine if an Achiever is in a job they hate where they're not recognized at all for their accomplishments. For them to stick with it, they'd need to make oodles of money or gain social status with the right people, both of which are things that *soothe* rather than *address* and *examine* that core fear.

What do you think this Three will do with the money they earn from this job that grossly undervalues them? Invest it soundly? Save it diligently? Or are they likely to fill those unmet emotional needs through spending their paychecks?

From the Achievers I've seen in this situation, nine times out of ten, an expensive, high-status car is in their future if they don't already own it. Or maybe a house with way more square footage than they'll ever need. Pricy art they don't understand or even like. A good-looking partner they can't stand. Maybe even 2.5 kids they don't enjoy spending time with and never really wanted. Threes (or anybody) who fall asleep to their deep emotional needs can easily end up playing this game they can never win.

That's not to say everyone with a fancy car, nice house, hot spouse, and kids is overcompensating for an unmet need or an Achiever. Please don't come at me. You know what I'm trying to say here. (Anyone who won't grant me generous assumptions this far into the book is invited to go away.)

However, if this same Three earns their money doing something that fulfills their core desire in a meaningful way and reminds them of their innate value as a human being, then they are much more likely to be in charge of their spending habits, rather than the other way around. They can use their money to usher their gifts into the world, to inspire others, and to blaze a trail for others to come after them. (Think: Oprah.)

Let's return to the question: what do you want your money to do for you?

Here are some examples:

"I want my money to open up options for me to explore and enjoy the world."

"I want my money to support the people around me when they need help."

"I want my money to keep me from having to sacrifice my morals just to pay my bills."

"I want my money to support me in my other intellectual pursuits."

Once you're clear on this, you might suddenly realize that you need a lot less money than you thought to accomplish your goal. Even small amounts of money from your books can fill you up a great deal.

Imagine if you want your money to support the people around you when they need help (without putting yourself out or having to play a martyr). This doesn't mean you must have enough to pay everyone's medical bills (this may only make sense to my American friends, but trust me when I say that's a lot of money). It can mean that, after you've paid your bills for the month, maybe tucked a little away for the future, you still have enough to take your friend out to coffee or dinner when she's had a bad day. And you can do it without thinking twice or expecting anything in return, because you're already getting what you need from the experience.

Now imagine if you want your money to create options for you to explore and enjoy the world. That doesn't mean it has to be enough for you to travel to another continent every month. Even having enough to go out and explore parts of your town or city that you've never seen can be fulfilling when you give it your full attention. That sushi place that everyone talks about? Go check it out. Close your eyes and sink into the flavors. Let the waiter recommend a sake pairing. Notice the satisfaction you gain from every small bite. A moment like that will fill you up both literally and emotionally, and it doesn't have to cost an arm and a leg. It doesn't take a lot of money to explore something new or enjoy the epicurean delights of the world, and when you've paid for that new experience with money from writing books you love and connect with, it'll taste even sweeter.

Here's what it boils down to: when you know what you want your money to do for you and you increase your money mindfulness, you respect each dollar so much more and experience true gratitude for every book you sell.

That leads to a meaningful career that can remain unaffected by the temptations of the next apparent gold rush. You don't need a million dollars (though you might end up making that) to be happy. You can be emotionally satisfied every day, with every sale. And that means you can make clearheaded decisions every day, so that five, ten years down the road, you're exactly where you want to be.

A FINAL WORD ON ENVY

I want to return to this topic once more. It's that important. When you're focusing on your career and minding your business, feeling envious of others becomes a nonissue. If you take away anything from this chapter, I would love for it to be that your career is truly unaffected by everyone else's career unless you make it so.

Publishing is not a zero-sum game. Someone else's success doesn't take anything from you. Someone else's failure doesn't give anything to you. Your career will be unique because you have unique talents and a unique voice, background, and way of moving through the world, even if you don't realize what that is yet. I've worked with a lot of authors, and I know this to be true.

So I'm not going to hit you with the "rising tide lifts all boats" thing, because I think that's nonsense. Why? Because it implies that your career is somehow reliant on all the other careers in this industry. Certainly the state of the industry can make particular tactics more or less effective, but in the end, you can write, edit, publish, and deliver your books to your readers whether the industry is booming *or* on life support.

Does this sound selfish? Am I telling you never to help your fellow indie when you see an opportunity? Never to collaborate on a project? Not at all. Both of those activities can supercharge your creativity and production and meet those core needs of yours in a healthy way. But learn what is yours and what is not yours first.

Robert Greene talks about envy in depth in his book *The Laws of Human Nature*, and reading his words was the first time I'd considered the concept and possible consequences fully. Once I gave the idea of envious personality types (not Enneagram, but more generally) some serious consideration, I realized not only how prevalent they are, but how absolutely devastating it can be when these folks focus their negative attention on you. There are very unhappy people in this industry (in Enneagram speak, these would be folks in low-average and unhealthy levels of development across every type). Their misery is not your fault and it's not your responsibility to fix that for them—and you couldn't if you tried because the solution is inner work that only they can do.

I don't want to catastrophize too much, but suffice it to say that those unhappy people can be extremely dangerous to be around. They don't want the best for you. Misery loves company. This isn't a new idea, but it's one many of us forget again and again (myself included).

The thing is, when you meet one of these people in real life, these envious personalities, sometimes you can pick up on it. If you tell them about one of your successes and for a split second they look unhappy, you probably don't want to keep going on about your successes in front of them. Or, conversely, if you talk about a failure, and they look pleased by that, you also probably do not want to spend that much time around them. And for god's sake, don't keep feeding that need of theirs by telling them about your failures. You might *think* you're being humble or helping by showing that you are imperfect, but in reality, you're feeding an unhealthy need of theirs and providing them fuel for criticizing you to others later, whenever they feel it will benefit them the most.

Listen to your gut on this one (or if you're a Five and don't naturally have easy access to your intuition, look at the data their face is providing). If you feel like putting yourself down is the best way to ingratiate yourself to someone, you don't need to be ingratiating yourself to them (and for my compliant Ones, Twos, and Sixes, just a reminder that you don't need to be ingratiating yourself to anyone). If you feel uncomfortable speaking frankly about the things you're grateful for around a person, be around that person less often or not at all. It doesn't mean they're bad, it just means they're not in a place to receive that information in a healthy way.

BUT! It's possible they will be later on, if they learn what they need to grow, so skip the guilt about putting them to the side *for now*.

The author community is spread around the globe. If you live in a big city, you may know a handful of other indie authors whom you can meet up with, otherwise most of your interactions within the community will take place online, specifically on social media. The problem here is that when you post your successes on social media, specifically the financial ones, you do not know who is seeing those numbers and what their immediate reaction is on their side of the screen. Are they grinning or scowling?

I have a tendency toward cynicism, so I tend to assume there are always more people who respond poorly to the success of others than respond with genuine glee.

The point is that when you post that sort of thing on the internet forever, you could have untold numbers of envious people homing in on you as the hot new target of their envy, and you would never know it.

Except you will know it, but only when it comes back to bite you in the ass. Because highly envious people lack the tools to lift themselves up, their only option for soothing their feelings of inferiority is to knock you down. They will go after your career if they can, and usually by attacking you as a person. They probably won't succeed, since part of being an indie author is that you only have to worry about your reputation with your fans, but they'll make themselves a pain in the ass anyway.

All this from one public post about financial success?

Yes. I've seen it happen. Many times.

I've been on the receiving end of it, too, most recently with the Kickstarter associated with this book. A necessary evil of that platform is that it shows how much money backers have pledged, and when envious personalities see that, all they see is a large number. You can bet they're not thinking of all the work that goes into fulfilling those promises.

For whatever reason, I didn't bother with concerns of envious people with the Kickstarter. Probably, I was too focused on the project to worry about petty matters like that. But envy doesn't take a holiday, and I didn't go unscathed.

(Would I do another Kickstarter, knowing that envy follows public money numbers? Hell yeah. Already have another in the works. That doesn't mean I'm going to post any *other* earnings numbers anywhere, though. I'm okay with the necessary evil of Kickstarter's setup, and I know what to watch out for with the envious personality trait.)

I'm not trying to scare you here (okay, maybe a little); I'm just trying to tell you the reality of what happens within *any* professional community. Ours is no different except for the fact that it is so highly *encouraged* to provide financial information. Posting exact information, stats, graphs, etc. is what will catch the attention of an envious person, whereas simply establishing something vague like "yeah, I'm able to pay my bills" is not going to attract quite the same negativity.

This is also one of the reasons I strongly encourage authors to go beyond mere networking and meet other authors whom you would go so far as to call friends (Twos, Sevens, and Nines do this without meaning to, but the rest of the types may need to make a conscious effort). I'm talking the kind of friends who will let you know if rumors start circulating about you, and may even go so far as to defend you before letting you know what's going on without your knowledge.

There are a few notable examples of leaders in this industry who share their yearly numbers openly, honestly, and altruistically, and I'm grateful to them for doing so. At the same time, people like Joanna Penn and Chris Fox, who offer these types of year-end recaps, have built up extensive networks of supporters over the years and have earned the respect of the indie community to the point where the sparks of envy that may arise aren't provided the oxygen they need to turn into a destructive fire. But I'm sure that hasn't always been the case, so I'm grateful to these folks who have faced the envy shitshow and persevered anyway.

Is this where you're at in your career, though? Have you given so much to this community that your goodwill has built you safety in every corner of the industry? If not, then I suggest you keep those numbers to yourself as much as possible, only sharing them with close friends (preferably in a mastermind with an NDA) who have proven themselves unlikely to fall into the envy trap.

Be picky. Share your success (whatever that means to you) only with those who will celebrate it. For one, you deserve it, and for another, when you commit to fulfilling work you truly love, the positive feedback you're seeking is baked right into the process.

COMPETING VALUES

What happens if you go through the process of establishing your creative and financial values only to find that you hold competing ones?

I say *if*, but really what I mean is *when*. It's inevitable. And that's because we don't just have one thing that we want in life. We have core desires and core fears, but we also have many other desires and plenty of other fears, and those influence how we live our lives as well.

Some people also have two types that are strong as far as the Enneagram goes (though only one is the dominant type), and you might feel like your runner-up manifests during certain situations.

We are multifaceted people.

For instance, my financial desire may look like wanting to have enough money to help the causes and the people that I believe in. But it would *also* be nice to have money to spend on extravagant vacations once a year. Ooh! And I'd love to never have to answer to anyone else again! And it would be sweet to be able to have enough money to retire early so that I could read more books before I die.

All of a sudden I have conflicting financial interests, don't I? They may not conflict at first, especially if I have a month that makes me $15,000 profit. I could contribute to all three of these desires that month. Well, maybe not retire, but I would feel good taking a few days off to read on the couch instead of my usual writing, consulting, and marketing. I could also afford a nice trip and hefty donations to some of my favorite charities.

But what happens when I don't have a $15,000 month? What happens when I pay off the expenses that I accrued that month for my business and only have a little bit left to pay myself? What I pay myself must first go toward bills and mortgage and all that other boring adult shit. Let's say that after I've done that, I have about $50 left. Where do I put that? Do I put that in a vacation fund? Do I donate that to a local charity? Do I use it to buy books to read over the weekend?

When the resource becomes scarce, then it's time to make a choice.

That's just one example of when these multiple values clash. If you can only choose one option, which would you choose? Or do you split your minimal resources between all three, and only get small returns from each?

I wish I had the answer for you, but the truth is that it's up to you to decide how to handle situations like this. I will tell you that whichever one tends to align more with your core desire is going to give you a bit more of an energy boost when you fulfill it, but there is something to be said for spreading your resources around and having a bit of variety. So, there's no right or wrong answer, it's just a matter of getting real with yourself about how each desire will play out, and how each option will or will not satisfy your immediate desires versus your long-term goals.

COMPROMISING YOUR VALUES

What happens when we compromise our core values?

This may seem like a question with an obvious answer ("we feel bad"), but it's important to walk through it anyway. Consider it a refresher, and one that we could all use, considering how hard society pressures and tempts us to compromise our values for whichever ones benefit those in power the most.

There are a few reasons why we might give in to this temptation. One is that we don't know what our individual values *are*; we haven't fully considered what matters to us at a deeper level. Another is that those around us have pressured us. Peer pressure doesn't end as soon as we graduate high school, though I wish it did.

The reason I see most often for this sacrifice, and am myself most tempted by, is for *short-term gains*. We say to ourselves, "I know this isn't exactly in line with my values, but it's short term, and it'll pay off big time. I can sacrifice my values for a short time for X benefit."

But can you? If it does pay off big time in the short term, what then? Are you *really* going to stop doing the thing that just paid off big time? Or are you more likely to try to turn that short-term payoff into a long-term one, or at least a series of short-term ones? "Yes, I compromised my values on this project, but I just had a $10k month when I usually never break $2k! If I just did this every month this year, I'd make six figures!" If you can imagine yourself falling into this trap, you're not alone.

That was the biggest danger for me earlier in my career. I would say, "I'm just going to work sixty hours a week in the short term, and it'll be worth temporarily sacrificing my health and my free time and my social life to make this much money."

I know it sounds counterintuitive, but the worst possible outcome of such a short-term sacrifice is that it works, and you make a lot of money. When that happens, you run the serious risk of that temporary sacrifice of values turning into a long-term one. Trust me when I say the long-term attempt at this only ends with you in shambles—exhausted, not living up to your own standards, probably experiencing serious health problems.

If the short-term sacrifice *doesn't* pan out, then we usually have a 50/50 chance of either saying, "I just have to do this a little longer to see the reward," or "I guess it doesn't work and I might as well return to my values." Failure sucks, but at least in this instance, we stand a chance of recentering our values.

Money doesn't solve all problems, but when you have money problems, it sure as shit solves those! And that's the kicker. Money is the greatest temptation for us to abandon our values because it does feel so good to have lots of it.

However, when your way of getting it sacrifices your values, money can become a flashy and slow poison.

I had to start asking myself, if I make the short-term sacrifice and it earns me a ton of money, how likely am I to give it up? Or am I more likely to turn it into my lifestyle?

(You know, until it runs me into the ground.)

That's one of the reasons an author would compromise their values to begin with. We justify it somehow, either with money or social status.

But what it looks like in the long term isn't pretty. It looks like chronic health problems, bitterness about the world, envy of others, depression, anxiety, marital problems, parenting problems, lost relationships with friends, low self-esteem—or many of these all at once.

The very best thing we can do is get clear on what those values are and stop trying to ignore them in the short term without expecting long-term negative effects. Instead, respect your values and begin viewing them as your strength. If you follow the map they lay out for you, you'll end up in a place where you're proud to be.

HOMEWORK

Answer the three questions:

1. What do I want my writing to do for me?

2. What do I want my writing to do for others?
3. What do I want my money to do for me?

Plan for the inevitable. Complete the following sentences with how you would prefer to behave in each situation:

1. When I notice my core fear being triggered, I will...
2. When I feel envy or comparisonitis set in, I will...
3. When I crave instant gratification, I will...

CHAPTER 4
WHAT IS MY PERSONA?

WHAT IS A PERSONA?

This chapter is all about how you show up in this career through your writing and author presence. It's a humongous topic, but there are some important questions you can ask yourself to make sure that whatever persona you do develop is one you can sustain for the long haul.

Last chapter, we covered your Creative Values. Now, we're going a level deeper to talk about your Persona.

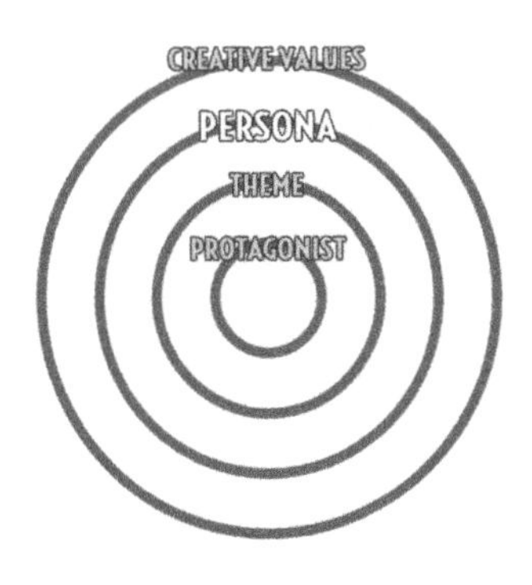

When I encourage you to intentionally define your persona, I'm not telling you to create the indie author version of Ziggy Stardust, but you could if you wanted to. Most personas aren't that complicated (or awesome?) because they don't have to be. Our ilk is already well versed in the concept of a pen name, so a persona is just a continuation of that thinking.

For example, pen names allow us to present a part of ourselves to our readers while protecting other parts of ourselves from public view. Sometimes that means obscuring our gender so we can defy gender norms and have readers see us as a *person* rather than solely as our gender. Some people think this is deceptive, but I'm not one of those people. If you live in a society that judges you unfairly for your gender, then it's society's fault for feeling betrayed when you take the necessary steps to avoid that unfair judgment, frankly.

It's also not uncommon for someone to pick a pen name that disguises their ethnic heritage when that particular heritage might similarly cause people to skip over the book for that specific reason. But you do have to be careful about this. When your race, ethnicity, gender, etc. is the cultural default and does not disadvantage you as a result of widespread social prejudice, then adopting the identity of someone from a marginalized group is a big no-no. There are plenty of thin-skinned people who've never had something be off-limits to them and want to claim that what I've just said is a double standard, but it's not, and I think most of us understand how the world works, so I won't belabor the point.

Sometimes people pick a pen name solely because they don't want their name forever tied to the books they're writing. Often this has nothing to do with shame and more to do with writing in a genre that the world will judge them for (or their boss would fire them over).

Sometimes pen names serve an even more practical purpose. I use pen names not because I'm ashamed of anything that I write but because I don't think that the readerships would cross over well, and I want to be able to best serve each target reader individually.

Each pen name is a brand. If Nike started selling orthopedic shoes, the consumer confusion could only be topped by Dr. Scholl's selling soccer cleats. *Could* each of those brands eventually communicate the message effectively to the target shopper? Sure, but it would probably take more time and money to communicate that message than it was worth, and loyal customers might be too upset or confused to stick around in the meantime.

Regardless, a persona is *more* than just a pen name. It's a whole vibe. It's also not a lie, or doesn't have to be, and probably shouldn't be if you're going to keep it up long term. Instead, it's a *filter*.

We are full-spectrum humans, but not every genre needs to see our full spectrum. That's why there are different genres. They allow writers and readers to instantly communicate what sort of things will be included in the story and what will not be included in the story. If you write a military sci-fi with zero romance in it, readers are hardly going to get mad at you for excluding romance; that wasn't what they were there for to begin with. In fact, you might *lose* readers by including it, since it is not usually an element they would expect.

Same basic concept goes for persona. You do your readers a great favor when you present them with an author persona that helps feed the fantasy you're selling them in the books. Readers appreciate this. Say you write westerns and you live in Arizona. Sharing pictures of the quintessential Arizona landscape, any antique pistols you might have, you in a cowboy hat, you on a horse—all those things will delight your readers. You shouldn't expect emails from them demanding to see you at a roller-skating rink, at a wine tasting, or letting your daughter put your hair in a dozen tiny ponytails. Sure, each of these things *could* contribute to a unique persona for a western author, but they're not going to be expected, per se.

I'd be remiss not to add that you're allowed to keep important parts of your life private. Period. You have permission—from me, from your doctor, from your god, from whoever. You are not obligated to tell your readers about your divorce or cancer scare or even your children you love so much. Building a clear persona helps you preserve these private parts of yourself while maintaining a public-facing life.

Going back to the full-spectrum metaphor, you are a rainbow. Everybody is. You shine light of every color in your daily life—gleeful, depressed, optimistic, pessimistic, eccentric, conventional. You've got a little bit of everything in you. You feel it, live it, probably worry about it every day. Certain colors of your light might be accepted or encouraged in one environment you love but discouraged in another. You feel comfortable letting, say, purple shine at church, but yellow when you're out with your friends at a rodeo. And there's nothing inherently hypocritical about this. (Though the best environments—and friendships—are the ones where you can shine with whatever color you are that day.)

Now let's look at your writing. You might only show your western readers those colors of yours that fall within the orange

range. But what if you also write techno-thrillers under a different pen name? It might not make sense to email your techno-thriller readers the same pictures or stories that you sent your western readers. They may not care about you on your horse, and your gunslinging may even offend some of them. Instead, you'll show your techno-thriller audience genuine parts of your life that reflect *their* shared interests, namely, techno-thrillers. You would show them all of your light within, say, the green range, and filter out the other colors.

This is the basic concept of an author persona. It's an overly simplified version, of course (don't worry, Fours, you don't have to feel emotionally stifled), but I want us on the same page before we move on. Because it can get much more complex (and potent) once we factor in your Enneagram type.

THE PERSONA DECIDES FOR YOU

Why is it strategically important to carefully and mindfully cultivate this persona? There are a few key benefits. The first is that it will help you connect to the *right* readers. The clearer your image, the more instantaneously readers will be able to say, "This looks fun," or "Hard pass."

I can think of few things more obnoxious than those negative reader reviews where they're upset because they essentially wanted it to be a different book from what you wrote. They leave me borrowing a quote from *Westworld* and shouting, "The maze wasn't meant for you!" at my computer screen. Even if you nail the genre with your cover and sales page description, a few of those lame reviews on book one of a series are inevitable because not everyone who can read can also think. But you don't want more than necessary. And to do that, you must warn off the wrong readers. Send them shrieking in the other direction!

A fear of those hard passes (Ah! Rejection! Exile!) keeps so many authors from creating clarity on that thing we call your "personal brand." Especially when you're starting out, you'll take whatever readers you can get, right?

Except when you try to please everyone, you risk strongly appealing to no one. (Also, you cannot please everyone, no matter how hard you try.)

Trust me, your relationships with the majority of your family and friends are better if they *never* read your books. If you have a cousin or bestie who is *really* into the genre you write, then maybe. But otherwise, let friends and family stay that. You don't need them for a career. They ain't gonna be among your thousand true fans, and it's unhealthy to want the creator–fan power balance infiltrating your personal life.

Here's something I firmly believe *and* have evidence to back up: with few exceptions, no matter how narrow your books' appeal, there are enough people who will dig it that you can eventually make a comfortable living writing just for those people. I've heard of some crazy niche series out there that just kill it because the author makes no bones about who they are, what they write, and who it is and isn't for.

There is one big exception here, and that's memoirs when you're not already a known entity. That's *very* hard to sell, even if you, like, lived in a gator's belly for a year or built an entire neighborhood of permanent housing out of duct tape. If you want to write that because you feel creatively compelled to tell your story—fantastic! There's such incredible healing in telling your story. I'm just saying it can be hard to make a full-time living off the royalties alone, no matter how far out you stretch your timeline.

And one last benefit of creating a strong persona, or "alter ego," is that it allows us to put it on and take it off when we need.

We often become a better version of ourselves when we write. I'm sure you've experienced this before. We tap into our courage, love, acceptance, vulnerability, connectedness, humility, and so much more without even meaning to. It just comes out. It flows *through* us. We love our protagonists, no matter what mistakes they make, and we're able to step into the hearts and minds of people we might normally distance ourselves from. We explore an entire world inside of ourselves, and in doing so, we can unlock our deep connection to the world around us. When we fall into the flow of writing, we can experience a liberation from our stifling ego.

Then we log our word count for the day, stand up from the keyboard, and go back to being our imperfect full-spectrum self, crankiness, selfish desires, and all.

Our work is a wonderful place for our best selves to shine through, but that doesn't mean you have to confess all your sins to your readers afterward. You're welcome to if you have a punishment kink, but think about how many works of art you've loved... until you saw too much of the creator's life. Depending on what you want to deliver to your readers through your writing, you might sabotage it by showing them what's inside your head between, say, two to five in the afternoon (if you maintain a standard sleep schedule, this is generally where your cortisol is at its lowest).

I've made plenty of mistakes of this nature. As a humor writer, it's a no-brainer what my readers want from me. They want me to make them laugh. So, what happens when I don't feel like making anyone laugh? What happens when I'm tired, pissed off, and would rather stab the keyboard than tap it (this is one of the reasons I write in the mornings rather than two to five in the afternoon)? What do I write? What do I post to social media when I'm feeling down and need a friend instead of a fan?

The correct answer is: nothing. I should write and post nothing. Not for H. Claire Taylor, at least. Maybe one of my other pen names with a different persona attached will resonate with whatever part of myself is flaring up just then, but my humor folks don't want to listen. That's what friends are for, to listen when I'm having a complete meltdown or a life crisis of the commonplace variety. Readers don't need to be privy to that (unless being a self-sabotaging mess is, in fact, part of your persona).

But, as I said, I've made many mistakes. I've posted more "real" things to my humor readers, and while a few of them were nice enough to engage with it, it never gets the response that my dumb jokes do.

What happens next is that I feel bitter. I'm not proud of that, but it's the first emotion that hits before I rein myself in. My inner monologue is something like, *They don't care about you. They just want you to be their little dancing monkey and make them feel better. They don't care that you're a living, breathing human. Screw them!*

That's intense, right? But if you've made the same mistake, then this is a familiar sentiment. And guess what? There's truth to it. At least in my case, my readers *do* want me to make them feel better. That's why they come to me. They know I can make them laugh and help them make sense of the world. If I promise them that but deliver one of my epic *Why do I even try when we live in a world on the brink of annihilation?* soliloquies, that's a serious bait and switch (unless I make it funny). They have a right to walk away from that.

Also, no, they *don't* really care about me. Not in the same way my friends and family do. And how could they? They don't know me personally. They're under no obligation to care about me beyond what I can do for them, which they pay me for, so... even-steven.

This is the trap anyone can fall into when they have a public presence. And if you publish books, you have a public presence. Sometimes when our readers love one part of us, we want them to love all of us. But they're under no obligation to, nor is it possible from that distance.

So, in that sense, being able to slip in and out of our alter ego helps us keep those two worlds separate without dishonesty or inauthenticity entering the picture at all. We can treat our careers like Mr. Rogers treated his sweaters and shoes. We can change out of our persona when we get home.

BEING AUTHENTIC

The #1 thing to keep in mind about your persona is that it must come across to fans as authentic.

Of course you, a person with an internet connection and at least a couple decades of lived experience, have heard this advice before. And it makes perfect sense because no one likes a liar.

Except... people do. In fact, a lot of people love liars. And I'm not just talking about fiction writers who are liars by profession, I'm talking about all well-known personalities. The thing is, we only love *convincing* liars. As soon as we sense the lie, we cringe.

Don't worry, this isn't a lesson on how to lie, per se. But I do want to talk about lies of omission. Because that's what a strong persona is. It's authentic, but it's also a massive lie by omission.

Think about it. Does Stephen King really murder people and do creepy shit like the characters in his books do? No. (Not that we know of or could prove in a court of law, at least.) But the guy gives off a creepy vibe nonetheless. It's even mentioned in a *King of the Hill* episode. Stephen King's persona has penetrated *other* entertainment, it's that powerful.

But that's not the whole picture of who he is as a person, because as we've discussed, each of us shines in a full spectrum of color.

You don't have to strain your imagination to understand that King is likely not a creepy person when he brushes his teeth or talks with his wife about the book he's reading. He's probably not creepy when he naps or when he's at the DMV, either. We just never see those parts of him.

(Admittedly, his persona has started to change since he's joined Twitter, and it somewhat weakens and muddles the image he's spent decades building. But hey, maybe he's just sick of it and rich enough to stop caring. When I have Stephen King money, I'll stop giving a damn about strategy, too. But until then...)

You can't write as many horror classics as King has without having a deeply creepy side to you. In that sense, we can say that his creepiness *is* authentic, but it's by no means the whole picture of who he is. It's *his* creepiness that appeals to *our* creepiness.

That's what we want to do as authors, find the right slice of ourselves to push to the forefront to connect with that same slice in others. It's not a part of us that doesn't exist or that we only wish existed, it's an actual part of our multifaceted personality that we highlight. This persona will leave out much of ourselves but is still genuine. It's our authentic lie of omission.

PICKING A PART OF YOU

How, then, do you decide which part of you to show? That comes down to whom you want to notice you. This is where most marketing coaches start using the word "avatar." Create an avatar of the exact person you want to attract. Define their age, gender, geographical location, politics, religion, where they shop, which social media they use, and so on, ad nauseum.

This is solid enough advice. Having an avatar that you not only market to but write for can be a fantastic tool. But again, *how* do you decide who that is? It's entirely possible to end up creating and marketing to an avatar you kind of detest in the name of profitability or genre expectations. I've seen it happen, and it sucks.

Here's where the alignment comes in.

Think about what part of yourself you love the most. What part of your personality are you proud of? Are you kind, brave, loyal, moral, witty, ambitious, or fun? What abilities do you want to show off? Do you write outrageous sexual tension? Maybe you know how to whip up page-turning espionage. What is the one thing that, when you look at your writing, makes you go, "Oh, that's fantastic!"

No need to play humble here; this is just between you and yourself for now. And if you find that you're struggling to pinpoint something, think back to the last compliment a reader gave you on your stories that made you feel genuinely *proud*. What was the compliment about? Did the story give them a break from reality? Did they want to be friends with your protagonist? Did they laugh their ass off? Did it keep them reading all night?

Assessing what kind of compliments fill you up can provide strong hints about which of your talents matter to you. That's because we generally don't think twice when people compliment parts of us we don't value. If someone tells me that my book made them laugh harder than they thought a book could, that's a legal high right there. I could glide on that for days if not weeks. But if someone compliments my rich and varied language? Meh. Don't care. (Also, I don't get that compliment because I value the inclusivity created by writing stories at a widely accessible reading level, even if the content is for adults.)

Give the modesty a break for the next few minutes and think about what talents you possess that you prize. Then ask yourself how you can let those shine and lead the way.

I'll wait right here while you do that. Take some time to figure that out before we go deeper on the subject.

SUPERFANS AND HATERS

Ready? Great. Now let's go deep. We'll say you have the sliver of you that you love picked out. It's time to figure out whom you'll attract.

In general, and I mean *general*, we're attracted to people who show qualities we wish we had. We admire the qualities we value. If your persona has you or your characters saying things that are generally unpopular or ahead of their time, you're going to attract people who admire that courage or your ability to think outside the box. If you and your books are funny, you're going to attract people who admire your quick wit. And if you write imaginative fantasy worlds, you're going to attract people who wish they could create escapes like that for themselves and respect your ability to create something out of nothing.

The more you hit your talent dead on the nose with your persona, the more you're going to see two types of people emerge:

1. **Superfans.** We love these people. They make careers. Superfans connect with you across social media platforms. They'll create an account somewhere just to follow you. They'll ask you when your next book is out, email you to check in if you go silent for a while, and demand merchandise.
2. **Haters.** We don't love these people, and it's usually best not to engage with them, but they can still get us free publicity. They're *envious* of that thing we do well, and they think they could do it better. Only, they don't. *hair flip*

The emergence of these two groups is a true sign that you've created a clear and potent persona. Haters are the price you pay for superfans. But superfans pay your bills.

It's natural to be worried about haters, but I encourage you to talk yourself down when those feelings emerge. Haters aren't that bad, even once they really get going. For the most part, they exist in your life only through the internet, and that means you can log off and be rid of them whenever you choose. Will they live inside your head still? Maybe, but they don't have to. You have control over that through a regular centering practice, which I recommend every author have anyway.

Not only can haters become a nonissue, but if you're smart about it, they can be useful.

You don't want just anyone reading your books. Trust me. You want the *right* people reading your books. And the inverse of that is that you don't want the wrong people reading your books. Haters can help keep that from happening. Most of the time, their criticism is silly, incoherent, or too vague to convey meaning, and none of that makes *you* look bad.

The kind of readers you're looking for won't be turned off by those kinds of haters, and it can often work as a billboard to pull in the right readers.

For instance, as you might have guessed, not everyone is a fan of my Jessica Christ series, a comedy about God's daughter who's born in Texas. There are people who hate that it even exists, that somebody (let alone a woman) had the audacity to write it. Most of the virulent haters have not read a word of it and make it known in their one-star reviews that they have no plans to. (By the way, if someone says they haven't read your book in a review on your book, you can report that to the platform for review; they've removed plenty of those from my books in the past.)

It would've been idiotic of me to believe I could write the Jessica Christ series and face no criticism for it, or that in hitting publish on those seven books, I *wouldn't* be inviting people to misquote Bible passages at me totally out of context for the next few years. But guess what? When people leave me those one-star reviews, they're also leaving me free publicity and fantastic copy for my marketing. That's because my persona for that pen name is geared toward people who really dislike those who quote Bible verses as a means of condemning others.

So, if nothing else, we get a situation of "the enemy of my enemy is my friend," and my ideal reader sees that I am the enemy of the kind of people that they also don't like. Therefore, I might be the kind of person they do like.

Those one-star reviews do that work for me. And every now and then I can take a screenshot of one and send it to my email list, and my folks get a big kick out of it. Like I said, free marketing.

But you don't need to write something as controversial as I do for the same principle to hold. A lot of the times the things that the wrong reader hates about your book enough to leave a one-star review are the things that your ideal readers will love. It could be something as simple as first-person narration, tone, only a light focus on science in your sci-fi, or even that your book reminds them of another well-known book that they didn't like. None of these are faults with your work. None of these are controversial elements. They're simply a result of a single work of art being unable to be all things at once. Readers may act like you've done it wrong by doing it your way (plenty of readers wish they could be writers but will never take that step, so they become critics instead), and let them. They're broadcasting the traits of your story, and because some people prefer sci-fi that's light on the sci or first-person narration or an angsty tone or the famous book similar to yours, these reviews are also free marketing.

ENNEAGRAM AND PERSONA

In the previous chapter, we discussed how your creative values might be influenced by your Enneagram type. Does this apply to persona as well, you ask?

One hundred percent. Each Enneagram type brings amazing gifts to the world, and when we let those shine, we attract the people who need them. So I suggest you let them shine in your persona.

Use both the factor of genre *and* the factor of your Enneagram type in building your persona, and you'll begin to truly stand out from the crowd. Don't worry, I'll explain more.

But first, I want to break down some of the gifts that each type brings when we're feeling uninhibited and fully ourselves. These are the parts of each type that are incredibly attractive, relatable, and genuine.

Here are the gifts of the Enneagram:

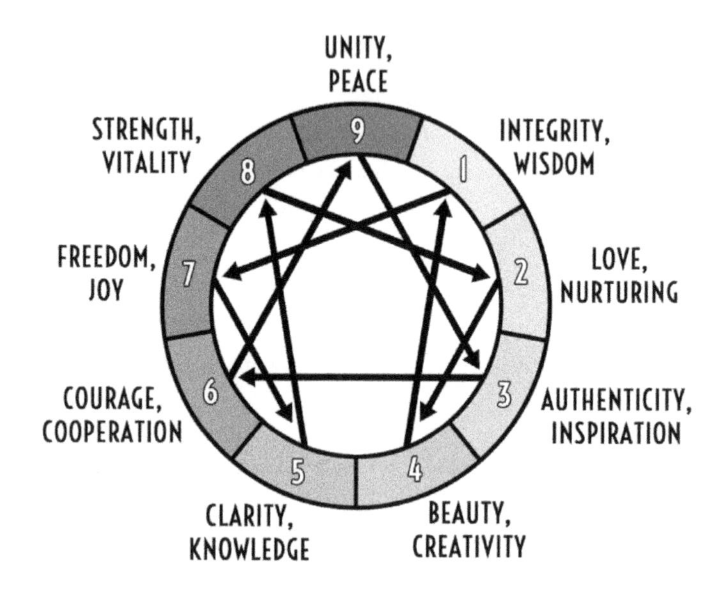

And here's a little more on each:

Type 1, the Reformer

If you're a Reformer, your unwillingness to tolerate immoral or unethical behavior is much needed in the world right now. Your supreme distaste for dangerous hypocrisy and your willingness to call it out at risk to your own reputation or safety will make you a refuge to people who feel like they're taking crazy pills every time they speak and act sensibly. There are a *lot* of irrational people out there, and your gifts of not only speaking truth, but living it, and possessing deep wisdom can be put on full display in any genre.

Ones are notoriously unpicky about which hills to die on—any and all look good—so maybe proceed with caution in this regard. But don't be afraid to call out injustice where you see it. Be the safe place for the rational and you might even start to change some people's minds (usually done through story rather than Twitter rants, just FYI).

Bonus: Because you're the type to think through all the moral implications before acting, when you let loose and have fun, your fanbase will be thrilled to join in, feeling sure that if you've already given it the seal of approval, they don't have to worry about it.

Type 2, the Helper

If you're a Helper, you are one of the sweetest people on Earth. For that reason, you've likely been treated brutally over the years by people who want to take advantage of that tenderness. But my God, we need more sweetness in this world! Be that. Be a nurturing respite for folks who need some gentle handling. Any genre can showcase your giving heart and gentleness, and when you do, you'll become the emotional oasis your ideal readers need.

One of your gifts is to anticipate the needs of others. You might occasionally wish you could turn that off, but in this case, you should play it up! You love to care for people, so nurture your readers. Ask them what's going on in their lives. Interact with them. If they get too clingy, you can always set boundaries, but in the meantime, you're going to deliver them a caring experience that many people can't find anywhere else. You don't need to be their therapist, but your emails and Facebook groups can feel like a safe place (you'll need to ensure this stays the case through clear rules and boundaries, but it's worth it, Two!).

Bonus: Your demonstration of nurturing *and* self-nurturing (yes, you must also do this) will inspire and empower your readers to turn around and do the same for themselves and the world.

Type 3, the Achiever

If you're an Achiever, you're the type of person who constantly hears, "Wow, how do you get so much done?" You possess a drive to achieve your goals that is almost superhuman. Your readers will flock to you for your ability to say you're going to do something and then do it. You strive to be better, and in doing so, you inspire others to admit they might want more out of life. Put simply, you motivate others just by going after what you want.

Now here's the bad news: your type faces the highest risk of accidentally being inauthentic. Have you ever wanted something so bad that you transformed yourself into the person you needed to be to get it? That's what I'm talking about here. This comes from your amazing talent at knowing what people want and then delivering that value, but if you're not careful, you will lose yourself in the pursuit. If you feel like your worthiness relies on selling 200k copies of your book in a year, that can become blinding, and you put yourself at risk of trying to be everything to everyone to get it done. Your readers *will* start to feel that desperation, and the reaction to that can be mistrust.

But with a little humility along the way, and if you're careful that your goals are deeply meaningful to you rather than chasing the empty carbs of arbitrary numbers or popularity contests, your ability to get shit done is going to inspire so many people to chase their dreams. When your readers feel like nothing's working in their favor, they'll always know they can come to you for motivation and *permission* to chase what they want and become who they want to be.

Bonus: When you share your failures with your readers, rather than revealing yourself to be a fraud, you'll be giving them a huge gift by showing that you can fail and still accomplish your dreams. You have the results to back up that claim.

Type 4, the Individualist

If you're an Individualist, I have great news for you that you're not going to believe. One of your gifts is helping people discover who they are. The reason you might not believe that is because there's a good chance you don't have a clear picture of who *you* are yet. But you're asking the right questions, and in asking those, and through sharing your introspective side and the messiness of your unique self, you'll inspire others to ask the big questions, too. You don't have to have it all figured out before you have something inspired to share.

Think about this: most people cling to fragile identities that prevent them from seeing the world as it is. I'm talking political, familial, ethnic, religious, and so on. Each of those identities can be shaken by outside forces. What happens to the person who always thought they were Chilean until their DNA test results told them they're Samoan (and adopted)? What happens to the mother whose children die? What happens to the devoted Christian when an elder in their church takes advantage of them? The answer is either cognitive dissonance or becoming terrifyingly unmoored. Regardless, it's messy. And that's where you come in. You demand deeper answers about identity and our place in the world. Even if you never find the answers, asking the questions creates a safe place for others to do the same. Helping others appreciate the disorganized beauty in themselves and the world around them is no small feat, and your unique outlook might be just the tool to dislodge them from the grip of social conditioning.

Bonus: Your weirdness (yeah, I said it) will provide a place for reluctant conformists to have some fun, be messy, and maybe be less conformist in the future. That's the kind of world you want to live in, right?

Type 5, the Investigator

If you're an Investigator, you have a wealth of knowledge to share with the world. Your observant nature is absolutely something you can delight your readers with through your persona. No matter what genre you write, there are related interests you can dive deep into then return with clarity and knowledge to share.

You may have the impulse to protect your knowledge or feel like you don't know enough yet to share with others, but I assure you this isn't the way to create a brighter future where fewer people act upon superstition and unchecked emotion rather than facts and reality. Trust me: when you get really excited about some topic or another, that excitement shines through to the right readers. Your stories will attract readers who care about accuracy and who like digging deep into topics, so all you must do for your persona to embody this is not hold back. Not everyone will share every interest you have right off the bat, but you have a talent for homing in on the fascinating parts, and when you share those, your readers will learn to trust that whatever you tell them will be worth their time.

This might sound counterintuitive, Five, but sharing your knowledge and inquisitive mind with others can bring you *more* energy. Not all communication equals depletion. Don't let your tendencies to bottle your energy stores in case of emergency stop you from connecting with your readers. You're not required to respond to every reader email, don't worry. Establishing yourself as the giver of information in the relationship and not the receiver is A-OK, but you might also be surprised what cool facts your readers can offer you. By broadcasting your knowledge, you might even attract experts farther along in the study who are just as engrossed in the topic as you are and want to share their understanding with you!

Bonus: Because you know so much about the topics you're passionate about, when you can simply express, "I don't know the answer! Experts are still trying to figure that out, isn't that cool?" you'll be modeling a positive learning behavior that 99% of the world doesn't know is an option, and that's saying, "I don't know yet... but I'm going to find out." Using your persona in this way could inspire untold numbers of readers to keep searching for truth rather than falling back on superstition or guesswork.

Type 6, the Loyalist

If you're a Loyalist, you have a special connection to possibilities. You're always thinking three steps ahead. Some call this anxiety, but in smaller doses, it's a gift. Your close connection to your own fear is a source of great strength. After all, an act isn't courageous if the person committing it isn't scared. You know that you can't take on the world alone, and for that reason, you value the social connections that keep us all safe. This understanding can lead to a sixth sense for cooperation.

Something to watch out for when relating to readers is letting your pattern of sorting the world into allies and enemies turn your fandom into an angry mob (pitchforks not included). Yes, there's safety in numbers, but courage usually stands on its own.

One of the gifts of your unique vantage point is that you live within arm's distance of your fear and have no problem naming it. And when you do that, your readers know they're not alone. Don't be afraid to share your fears, however irrational they may seem, with your readers. Sixes can mine a lot of humor in this topic, especially with the more irrational or over-the-top fears. When you can laugh about it, you free up your readers to laugh about it, and there's no tool quite like humor to master our fears. In a paradoxical way, and so long as you don't get too into the weeds on catastrophizing, talking about the things that scare you gives readers permission to feel and acknowledge the essential fears of life rather than pretending they don't exist. If you've ever been called neurotic (just taking a shot in the dark here, Six), it's time to reframe that, embrace your attention to detail and ability to forecast the future, and share that with the people who will embrace it.

One thing I know about you is that you value courage and despise cowardice, so let this be the thing you inspire in your readers through your persona. Spread the essential message of "I know you're afraid. So am I. We must do the brave thing anyway."

Bonus: When you inspire courage in others, the world becomes a safer place for all.

Type 7, the Enthusiast

If you're an Enthusiast, you have what I think is the most underrated type on the Enneagram. People come to you for a good time, but they often view your gift of joy as a bonus or a diversion, rather than the essential part of life that it is. And sure, a good time can be a simple diversion if there's no substance behind it, but you don't *just* enjoy the good parts of life—you find ways to make the tough parts tolerable. Your hope can be knocked down, but it never stays down. That's not your nature.

Readers will come to you for that sense of joy, of freedom, of flying effortlessly despite the harsh winds of your life. While I encourage Sevens to make time for stillness and to face the pain they would do anything to avoid, their persona doesn't need to include that, as it's the behind-the-scenes work for an Enthusiast.

Sevens, you get be your readers' escape. Yes, bad things must happen to your protagonist for there to be an interesting story, but you'll be able to raise your characters up again and show that transcendence is possible and that fun, faith, and joy can be found in the darkest of places.

Bonus: By prioritizing joy and endless possibilities as something you share with your readers, you'll find people who love the things that you love as much as you do. You'll also give yourself a valid business reason to go explore the world more fully (can you say "tax write-off"?).

. . .

Type 8, the Challenger

If you're a Challenger, you've had people tell you to dial it back your whole life. You've been called bossy or stubborn or a bitch. Or, if you're a man, you've been called a natural leader. As a writer, you can make this your persona. Be bold and opinionated for the people who don't feel like they can be. Be a courageous leader for your readers. There's no rule that your fanbase must run as a democracy. You make the rules. This is the place where you reign, and part of your responsibility is protecting your following. They will appreciate that strength and decisiveness or get lost. And what you'll be left with is your little utopia where no one can tell you what to do and everyone respects you. Hell yeah!

You will need to commit to being benevolent, though, and behind the scenes, you'll want to work on increasing your tolerance for your own vulnerability. Even you aren't immune to the power going to your head, and the last thing anyone wants it to become the thing they hate. But as long as you can stay strong while showing the Eight's virtue of kindness (best not to intimidate and scare the people who pay you), your fans will know they're in good hands, and when they need to read stories about a modest farmer from the outskirts taking on the abusive powers that be to protect the average folk, your stories will be a perfect place to find that, since you can't help yourself (and you shouldn't stop yourself from writing about these kinds of themes!).

Bonus: Your willingness to call out abuses of power you see in the world is a much-desired voice in our modern age of extreme inequality and people sucking up to, say, billionaire space cowboys. When people say, "Tell me how you *really* feel," you can do just that. No more worrying about losing your job. (Cancel culture doesn't exist in indie publishing; there's always a way to continue to put books on the internet and have people buy them.)

Type 9, the Peacemaker

If you're a Peacemaker, you feel a deep connection with and throughout the universe. Any two humans seem more the same than different. I'm here to tell you that your experience and view on this is *not* shared by most of the types. It may be the objective truth of the universe, but no one else feels it on an instinctual level quite like the Nine. When someone speaks with you, they leave with the impression that you agree with them and see things from their perspective, whether you do or not. You make people feel seen and heard, and so long as it's not at the cost of erasing parts of yourself to make more room for them, that's an invaluable contribution to the world.

Nines have an unending optimism about humanity that they often wish they could kick, but can't. And please don't, Peacemakers. Instead, use this in your stories to illustrate your generous view about humanity to people who have become cynical. Your objectivity and ability to show all sides is what earns you the title of the Peacemaker, and, boy, doesn't this world need a little more understanding of the "opposing" sides right now?

Even as your objectivity and fair-handedness annoys some people who are caught in their reptilian brain and urging false dichotomies of "you're with us or you're against us" and "if you're not part of the solution, you're part of the problem," kowtowing to that nonsense is not your purpose in this world.

Let the other types die on whatever hill they choose. There are plenty of people in the battle. Every war needs diplomats to end it, and that's where you come in, if you're willing to step into the fray. Through your persona, show how everyone has good in them and that angry people are usually just hurt people. Give yourself permission to protect the space of your stories and your platform as a place where people can come when they're tired of the cynicism and need to restore their faith in the world and feel connection instead of separation.

Bonus: Your generous belief in humanity and your identification with all people lends itself to writing deliciously complex antagonists. Lean into that. Don't be afraid to humanize them and challenge the reader to sympathize with someone who they normally wouldn't.

No matter your type, there is a crucial need for your gifts to shine through. Not everyone will be looking for the same thing in an author and their stories, but all of these gifts are required for the totality of the human experience to be seen, heard, and felt.

When you fail to consciously build an aligned persona, you deprive the world of what you have to offer. But when you spend time on this aspect of your career, you become a beacon that calls to the right readers in the right time of their lives and delivers exactly what they need.

HOMEWORK

1. Describe the part of yourself you want to highlight. What are some of your best qualities that you want to put into your writing?

2. What was the last compliment someone gave you about your writing that felt amazing to receive? What aspect of you was highlighted? Is this something you can lean more heavily on or a quality of your persona you might have overlooked?
3. Who do you *want* to impress? Who are your books for?
4. What's your plan for when (not if) painful criticism is lobbed at you? How will you react? What approach will you take? What actions do you consider off-limits?

CHAPTER 5
WHAT ARE MY THEMES?

WHAT IS A THEME?

This chapter is what your stories will be about. No big deal. It's the next level down in our circles, and my aim in this chapter is to make the sometimes-obfuscated topic of theme as simple and second nature to your storytelling as possible.

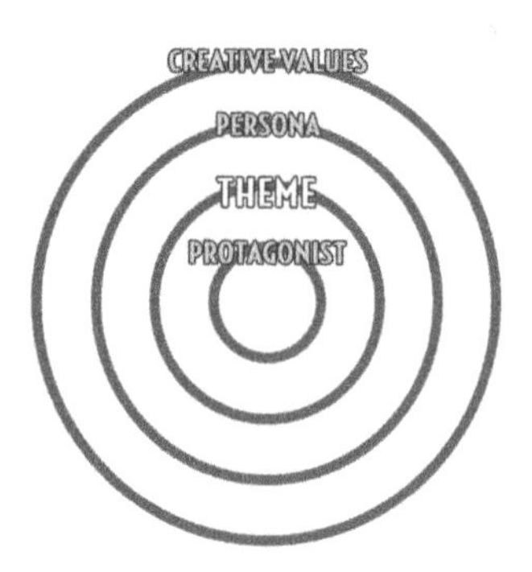

When I was in high school and college, and my teachers and professors explained to me what a theme was, it never really took. I can't explain it. They just kept saying "theme," and I kept nodding along and having no clue. It didn't help that they defined it in different ways, but also, *none* of the ways made sense to me. (One of my writing professors would demand we "pin down the four corners of the story" in every single workshop, and I'm guessing this was his way of talking about theme. Now, perhaps, you see why I was so confused.) The result of all this was that, for years, I decided to not worry about theme.

I don't recommend this approach. Neglecting theme makes everything harder than it needs to be in your writing, not easier. But if you don't know what theme is, you have little choice but to ignore it.

A shocking number of people in the indie author community contend that you don't need to think about theme at any point in your storytelling process, as if a theme is some sort of luxury or a sign of pretentiousness that's better left to literary fiction.

That is 100% untrue, and I will stand by that assertion Till the Bitter End.

Harry Potter has a theme.

Every Disney movie has a theme.

A Song of Ice and Fire has a theme.

Dan Brown novels each have a theme, for crying out loud!

Theme is what your story is about. So, if your story is about anything (strongly suggest you make sure that it is), then you have a theme in it whether you mean to or not. Probably multiple themes, and probably none of them fleshed out to a satisfying extent, if you don't pay them conscious and educated attention.

It's vital that you know what those themes are so you can run the story and the story doesn't end up running you. I'm not saying you should never lose yourself in the story, because that is one of the more pleasurable experiences of writing and why many of us do it. Feeling your sense of self melt away and becoming one with your fictional universe is great. In fact, it's a little orgasmic, and it's far cheaper than street drugs.

That being said, the story wants you to lead it. It is *your* story. There is a reason that story came into *your* head. Claiming that the story is in control and you can't tell it what theme to have isn't relishing the experience of storytelling, it's abdicating responsibility.

Here's the great thing: you can decide *when* you start taking theme into consideration in your writing process. Would it work better for you to decide on one during the outlining stages? Or maybe you want to discover it organically in your first draft and then flesh it out in revisions. You can publish a book with a strong and developed theme no matter when in your process you settle on that theme. That means that developing a clear theme can work for everyone, no matter where they fall on the pantser-plotter spectrum.

Personally, I hate wasted words. Cutting scenes, though sometimes necessary for the story, drives me crazy. I'm an incredibly busy person, and knowing that I wasted a whole morning on a scene that I trashed makes my eye twitch. Cutting scenes becomes a much more common occurrence if I don't know what my theme is prior to writing my first draft. It may be a fun scene, but if it doesn't move the story forward by advancing the theme-based conflict, then it tends to feel like a spare part and brings the pacing to a halt. I don't want any of that in my stories, because I like for readers to keep turning pages rather than setting the book down, so I've learned over the course of the dozens of books I've published that the best thing for me and how I want my writing process to go is to settle on a theme early.

But I also know this is not how many writers creatively thrive, so find where theme consideration works best for you.

Theme is the pulsing heart of a story. You can't remove it or neglect it and expect the tale to thrive or even survive.

But what is it? I still haven't explained this fully.

As I mentioned earlier, **the theme is what your story is about.**

Let's define that further. If I ask you what your story is about, I'm not looking for an answer like "It's a story about high school." Sure, that's where it's *set*. That gives us some idea about the age of the characters. But I was an athlete in high school. You might've been a theater kid or an outcast or an exchange student. There are all kinds of experiences happening in high school, so not only is this *not* what I mean by a theme, saying "it's a story about high school" is an incredibly vague *description*. You take any three adults and ask them about their high school experience, and you're going to hear three vastly different stories that would likely have three vastly different themes.

Let's go deeper on this high school story to find its theme.

What elements of the high school experience might feel more universal? What emotions? What fears and insecurities?

I don't have to tell anyone that high school is an emotional experience, no matter which club or team you were a part of. That age is an almost entirely emotional experience (although one could argue that it's no more or no less of an emotional experience than everything in our lives; we just had less control over our emotions, or believe we did, at that age).

I would bet that at various times in our high school experience, we each felt lost, lonely, joyful, devastated, heartbroken, anxious, ecstatic, humiliated, courageous, and very, very horny.

So, if I asked you what your story was about, and you said, "It's a story about the loneliness of being a young adult," I would point at you and say, "Yes! Much closer! But not there yet."

You can distill that even further. Because is loneliness as a teen really that different from the loneliness we experience as adults? It may result from other external stimuli, but the deep and persistent ache is the same.

I ask again what your story is about.

"It's about loneliness."

Bravo! We have a theme.

The theme is: loneliness.

What I talk about when I talk about theme is a single word. (Shout-out to the one professor who defined it this way for me, even though I was way too confused about theme by that point to understand. I get it now; it just took a while.)

Theme is the concept at the heart of your story, and you can do *so much* with it. You think adults can relate to a story about loneliness that's set in high school? Hell yeah! Adults read YA all the time, and the reason it remains accessible to us old folks is because we connect to the *themes*, which are universal and ageless.

FINDING YOUR THEME

Let's try this again.

I ask, "What is the story about?"

An author answers, "It's a bad-boy romance about a young upstart and her curmudgeonly boss."

Not a theme. Yet.

I reply, "Go deeper. What is the story really about?"

Author says, "Huh?"

But after a few minutes of thinking, they come up with "This is a story about a woman trying to find her place in the world after a bitter rejection."

Ooh, now I'm intrigued. We're going deeper. And maybe that's poor word choice when we're talking about bad-boy romance, or maybe it's *perfect* word choice.

But we're not done yet, because the author can distill this idea down even further.

It's a story about a woman trying to find her place in the world after a bitter rejection, so what does that boil down to when you take away the spare parts? What concept is at the heart of searching to rebuilt after rejection?

The answer is: it depends on the author's original intent, that is, what emotion or question prompted her to write the story in the first place. There's no single correct answer for what theme a story with this *premise* should have, so it's up to the author to decide which way they want to take it.

You could distill it down to a story about *rejection*. Or a story about *rebuilding*, or *identity*, or *resilience*, or *independence*. Each of those concepts is a strong theme to explore.

Now suddenly this bad-boy romance with a cranky boss and a young new hire is not only off-the-charts sizzling, but at its heart is a story about, say, *resilience*. And that theme is one hell of a platter upon which to serve your readers a delicious treat.

Not only will they get the romance tropes they love, but they'll hit "The End" feeling deeply connected to your heroine through their own lived experience of resilience.

WHAT'S IT GOOD FOR?

Why do we need a theme? Notice that I didn't ask if we need one. We've already established that this is one of the many hills in this hilly landscape of storytelling that I will happily die on. You need a theme. Not only that, but your story will have *at least* one theme emerge, no matter how hard you try to keep it at bay. So, it's a matter of deciding if you want a clearly developed and refined theme, or if you'd prefer allowing a few muddied themes to crop up, confuse the purpose of the story, lack emotional resolution for your readers, and leave you scratching your head as to how in the world to end the book or series in a satisfying way.

Personally, I prefer writing to be fun experience rather than an anxiety-inducing one, but you do you.

Actually, don't do you on this one. Write to a damn theme. Please, I beg of you.

The reason this is so important goes back to why we, human beings, crave stories.

We all receive roughly the same data as we move through the world. The sun is warm, the grass is green, waiting in line sucks, citrus fruits can be delicious but a little bit challenging, and it feels great to laugh. With very little variation, we are all working from those same data points of reality.

So where do all the miscommunications come from? Why doesn't everyone agree about the way the world works?

The trouble comes from the *meaning* we assign to these data points, and the connections and relationships we draw between them.

Accepted premise: sunshine is warm.

Quest for meaning: Why is the sunshine warm?

Possible answer: Because it's made of fire, and fire is hot.

Possible answer: Because God made it that way when she was in a bad mood.

Possible answer: Because it's working up a sweat holding all the planets in orbit.

Or if you're stuck in traffic and your small child keeps asking questions like this, the answer might be "Because it is, okay? Ask your teacher tomorrow."

It's basic survival instinct to encounter something with our five senses and ask, "What does it mean?" Is it a friend or foe? Do I need to fear it or pursue it? This type of information has allowed us to survive as a species.

And then this thing called personal identity evolved in us and essentially fucked up everything. Suddenly we were asking questions about *our place* in the world. We went from "I am here and I would like to not die," to "Why am I here?" The understanding and meaning we sought became much broader and much more complicated (even impossible) to gain through empirical means. As a social species, we began to read meaning into every action of those in our group to determine where possible threats of exile might lie so we could make things right before that happened.

Imagine the first caveman to ever ask his female mate, "Are you okay?" only to receive an unconvincing "I'm fine." He had objective data points to work from, but he had to figure out how they connected meaningfully or risk her finding the next hairiest guy in the region to bump clubs with.

(This is obviously a cartoon version of reality, but you get my point.)

We're desperate for lessons and tips about the important concepts we experience as humans, like loss, fear, ecstasy, and forgiveness. We want to survive and thrive and feel successful and that our lives have meaning, and all our messy emotions make those goals difficult if we don't understand how to process them. We need tools! We need knowledge! We need wisdom! We need comfort!

We need meaning!

And your theme is the decoder ring for your story's meaning. It's what signals that there is a point to the story, and that the reader will gain some valuable insight into themselves, others, or humanity at large if they stick with it.

Civilizations around the world have relied on stories passed between generations as teaching tools for the body, mind, and spirit since time out of mind. As western cultures have begun to silo each generation more and more, that flow of information has slowed to a drip for many, many people. If you're like me, you never spent time around your grandparents. Even my time with aunts and uncles was limited to a few visits where I stayed out of sight because they were boring adults. The point is that growing up, I had to find other sources for information about the world.

J. R. R. Tolkien, the patron saint of Type 6 Loyalist writers, taught me lessons about *courage* and *loyalty*.

The American Girl series showed me the value of *resilience* and *identity*.

The tales of Edgar Allan Poe, a Type 4 Individualist, provided insight into *fear* and *jealousy* and *obsession*.

And the Chronicles of Narnia by C. S. Lewis, a Type 1 Reformer, taught me the about *integrity* and *faith*.

It should be noted that the Chronicles of Narnia didn't convert me to some form or another of Christianity (I remained a little heathen child), but the themes of the seven books still resonated undeniably with my Reformer core motivations and showed me the value of respecting and living by the set of moral rules I'd already constructed, as well as the importance of developing them more fully.

I'm sure the adults in my life said things to the extent of "It's important to be brave, Claire," or "Always act with integrity," but what they didn't do was tell me fascinating tales about elves and badgers and immigrants and orangutans that captivated me, connected, and *showed* me what they meant.

And none of those stories would've meant a damn thing without a strong theme tying the pieces together, adding meaning to the data points of plot.

A golden ring could represent any number of things, but when it can bestow unlimited power, and you carry it to a volcano to destroy it with the help of your bestie, that golden ring suddenly says a *particular* thing about what it takes to destroy unjust power in this world.

We crave knowledge of universal truths about loyalty and compassion and goodness, because then, once we know the truths (or believe we do), we feel like we have some power over the chaotic world. It brings us a sense of massive relief to think that we may understand something about our environment.

That's why the initial creative sparks of most great stories occur when the author encounters something that doesn't make sense and that they can't categorize, or when they have their own breakthrough and want to share it with the world.

None of this is to say that in developing a strong theme, you'll avoid readers misinterpreting your work. I wish that were true, but no matter what you do, someone will misinterpret it. Still, theme is a nice guide for the reader to think about the events and possibly come up with the same conclusion that you did.

As to the question of why stories need themes, it's really a two-parter. Part 1 is that the storyteller benefits from exploring a single theme in depth to some sort of satisfactory conclusion, and knowing the theme allows the author to know *where* the story ends. Part 2 is that the reader benefits from the ride the author takes them on while exploring this theme.

In that sense, theme unites the experience and understanding of the author and the reader, the sender and the receiver, and I struggle to think of any more important connection between two people than a shared understanding of the world.

THEME AS A SINGLE WORD

As you might have caught by now, I prefer to think of theme as a single word. This is in part due to theme equaling a concept, and concepts are usually single words. "Trust" is a concept. But an exception can be made for something hyphenated like "self-respect" (or you could simply go with "respect"). The point is not that it is one word; the point is that your theme is a concept that lends itself to exploration.

Deciding on a single word helps crystallize the theme in my mind while opening it up for the greatest possible exploration. By using a single word like *courage* or *belonging* or *grief*, we start with a single data point and no context in which to interpret it or other data to which we can connect it. Yet.

Any single data point begs for a connection because the connections make the context, and only with the context can we assign the meaning our human brains crave. A single data point is logically useless, even though plenty of people on Twitter are happy to take a single data point, a single news story, and assign it plenty of context to reinforce their existing views on the world.

But people with basic critical thinking skills and a modicum of emotional intelligence will easily understand that nothing can be learned from a single data point, and that is what our theme is. It is a dot floating in nothingness.

Our story, then, creates the context.

Take, for example, the theme of *courage*. There is a standard definition in the dictionary for the word, so we can know the *denotation* of our data point. But ask two people for an example of courage in action, and you might be shocked by how different their interpretations of the word look when provided real-world context.

The contexts they choose might look vastly different, too. What does courage look like in the context of your family? What does courage look like in the context of your profession? What does courage look like in the context of a tumultuous romantic relationship?

And outside of general contexts, there are all kinds of *questions* we can ask about courage. When is courage quiet? When is courage bold? What happens when courage fails us? How should we proceed when others fail to be courageous on our behalf?

These are all big questions to explore, and here's the kicker: you can explore them in *any genre* you choose. That's because genre exists in the realm of the *external*, and our theme forms the internal world—the protagonist's emotions, values, and beliefs. That internal world then causes the protagonist to take actions in the external world, at the plot level. But it all starts from the inside, at theme, and moves outward, toward genre and plot.

Our theme not only helps us form the core of our story, it is one of the most fantastic tools in our author toolbox to make *decisions* about our story. If you're ever unsure what to write next, look back at your theme. Your protagonist feels some way about it, but over the course of the story, their beliefs will be changing. (That's what a story is, your protagonist is knocked off balance and struggling to get their feet under them, experiencing change along the way.)

So, if you don't know what to write next, you can ask, "What needs to happen *externally* to force my protagonist to continue their *internal* development with regards to the theme?"

For example:

"What do I need to do to Sally (protagonist) to force her to confront her fear of responsibility (theme)?"

Protagonist: Sally, probably a Type 7 Enthusiast.

Theme: Responsibility.

Sally's original belief (theme statement): Responsibility will inevitably trap me in an unpleasant situation and is not worth the rewards it could provide.

There are many answers to what we could do to Sally to make her reconsider and redesign her original belief about responsibility. Maybe her aunt dies and leaves her a chipper dog to care for. You can already see how this might teach Sally that some responsibility can make life richer and *more* liberating. (Dogs or doglike creatures [I see you, sci-fi and fantasy authors] are the cure for what ails any story, in my opinion, but I'm also a total dog enthusiast, so I am biased.)

The point is that knowing the theme and your protagonist (we'll cover protagonists more in the next chapter) is all you need to start asking the right questions to free you from a boring or stuck scene.

I have what some might call an addiction to Post-it notes, but you don't have to be an addict like me to use this next tip: write your theme in bold letters on a sticky note, and stick it to your computer monitor. Put it at eye level. When you're not sure how to proceed, check back in with that and ask yourself how you can advance that theme or further explore it to challenge your protagonist's current beliefs.

Here's another important note: your theme should always hit on an internal (emotional/philosophical) level as opposed to an external (physical/superficial) level.

For instance: baseball, winter, Connecticut, and red are not themes. They are one word each, sure, but they touch on the external and do not leave much room for different contexts. Connecticut might be a fine *setting*, as might winter, but they are not themes. *Love, Actually* was not a movie about Christmas (setting), it was a movie about love, actually. The reason that movie feels like a single movie and not twelve different movies is not only because the stories intertwine with one another, but because every story shares the same theme. That's what ties them together.

Does each subplot of *Love, Actually* explore love in the same *context*? Not at all. That's why I can ship the Colin Firth storyline so hard (all cringy power dynamics aside), and shout at the screen every time Laura Linney's character can't *mute her fucking phone* to hook up with Carl at least *once*. I don't like her verdict on the theme of love (choosing codependence over possible happiness), so that storyline will forever drive me up the wall.

Eh-hem. Anyway. A strong theme appeals to both our emotions and our values and/or beliefs. Our emotions interact with the *emotional conflict*, and our values and beliefs interact with the *philosophical conflict*. Together, the emotional and philosophical conflicts make up the "internal conflict" of the story. So, when people talk about internal conflict, they're speaking of both these things, and it's important that we, as storytellers, are aware that there are two types of internal conflict so that we don't neglect either.

Let's look at one more example. Say that *loneliness* is your theme. Does it hit at an emotional level? Definitely. Ouch. At the philosophical level, we would ask questions like "What is the point of loneliness, or does it even have a point?" "Can we benefit from loneliness?" "What is the difference between being lonely and being alone?" Notice that these are questions of meaning.

Meanwhile, if you pick a theme of *baseball*, first, you didn't pick a theme. But okay, let's try to imagine this: does baseball hit on an emotional level? I was raised by a father who made me sit down and watch baseball with him, and I can tell you, baseball itself may *elicit* emotions, such as excitement—or in my case, restlessness—but it is not itself an emotional or philosophical concept. I know, *mind-blowing*. Wow, Claire. This book should've been at least ten times more expensive for this kind of precious information.

But look, we still haven't touched the philosophical aspects of your theme of baseball. Can you ask, "What is the deeper meaning of baseball?" I mean, you *can*, but if you ask a question like that often enough and to enough people, you're going to start worrying your friends and family, and you might end up in a mental health facility. Not an optional one. Meanwhile, if you go around asking everyone, "What is the meaning of loneliness?" they'll just assume you're a poet.

To recap, yes, you need a theme, I highly recommend you boil it down to one word, and you do that by asking yourself, "What is the story about?" Then, when you give the wrong answer, meaning one that's too surface-level, ask yourself what is this book *really* about? Maybe then you have something like "This is a story about finding a place you can call home." Okay, we're getting very close now. What word is the underpinning of that question that you want to explore? And remember, there are a lot of possible answers here, and none of them are wrong. It's just a matter of which one you want to spend your time exploring.

Already we're at: "This is a story about finding a home for yourself." A theme that might go with that is *belonging*. This is a story about *belonging*. Once you've boiled it down to that single data point, you can start reaching out in all directions to pull in other data to create context. Within the context you create, your story will ask questions like "What does it mean to belong?" "How do we find belonging?" "Are there people who just don't belong?" "How do we make others feel like they belong?" "Are there certain groups that it's bad to belong to?" "Can you even belong to a group?" and so on and so forth.

Now it's your turn to start thinking about your story's theme. And from there, you'll build out your theme statement.

THEME STATEMENT

We each hold personal beliefs about concepts like *courage* or *loneliness* or *loyalty*. Sometimes the belief is conscious, but just as frequently, it's an unexamined unconscious belief that we picked up somewhere in early childhood or through the school of hard knocks. Maybe our caregivers modeled it or vocalized the belief explicitly, or maybe we developed the belief as a coping mechanism for trauma.

When dealing with subconscious and unexamined beliefs, it's not usual for us to maintain *more* than one on a single concept, and sometimes those beliefs contradict one another, creating cognitive dissonance. Thankfully, *that* never manifests in bizarre and harmful behavior.

These beliefs about the world are interlocked with our values. Our beliefs and values determine how we feel about what's going on in the external world around us. They influence our emotions. Our actions, then, are a result of a complex interplay between what's happening to and around us, what we think it means, and how that makes us feel. And what's true in human psychology for us living and breathing beings is true for your characters.

The protagonist of your story will have (possibly conflicting) beliefs about the story's theme. It's crucial to figure out what those beliefs are for your protagonist at the beginning of their story. And it's just as important to know how those beliefs evolve over the course of the story (at the book level *and* the series level).

That's what the story is, a progression of those beliefs changing based on new information that your protagonist is encountering. At the start of your story, page one, they have a faulty belief that but for the grace of God hasn't been blasted to smithereens yet. We all have those. They sustain us for a while, maybe help us feel safe or superior in a hollow sort of way, and then events in the world around us make it impossible to maintain that belief any longer without falling deep into denial or conspiracy.

So, at the start of the story (the "exposition"), it's important to show your readers how your protagonist *feels* about the *theme* based on *beliefs* and *values* they hold about that theme. This way, readers have an anchor point from which to chart the change in those values and beliefs.

The initial belief by your protagonist is what I call the "theme statement." It is, quite literally, a statement of belief your protagonist holds about the theme. Pinning this down can make the rest of your story flow much more coherently, but it does take a second to pause and flesh out.

Say the theme is "vulnerability." Your protagonist's theme statement might be something like "Vulnerability is weakness," or "If you're strong enough, no one can hurt you." Maybe the belief is overt, in that they know they believe it, intentionally build their life around it, and express it frequently to others. Or maybe it's a covert and subconscious belief, so they don't realize that their lack of vulnerability is what's destroying their relationships and creating the need to armor up, rather than it being the thing keeping them safe from harm.

Then here comes the inciting incident, fully ready to blow that flawed belief right out of the water. The inciting incident is the moment when the protagonist's theme statement stops working for them to the point where ignoring the dysfunction (which they might try to do for a while) causes big-time problems. The only thing that can restore their emotional equilibrium is adjusting their belief, and there are few things as agonizing in this world as that.

Think of the last time you changed a deeply held belief. It was not a painless process, was it? Maybe some of you never have altered or replaced a deeply held belief, and if that's you, I imagine your life is a bit of a mess. None of us get it all right from childhood, and that's that. The same is true for your protagonists. Everyone has faulty beliefs that need to be adjusted, corrected, or straight up thrown out.

When I work with authors on the start of their story, there are two things we need to know before forging ahead: what is your protagonist's theme statement, and what happens to blow that belief to shit?

Here's another example: let's say you're writing a book with the theme of *compassion*.

At the start of the story, your protagonist might provide a theme statement like this: to be a compassionate person requires helping everyone who needs it, no questions asked.

Great! Now we need something that blows that belief to shit. Maybe too much is asked of your protagonist and she must choose *who* gets her compassion because she can't help both people. Or maybe her compassion is abused by someone she trusted. Or maybe in acting compassionately, she enables someone instead of helping them. Now she must re-examine what she believes about compassion over the course of and throughout the events of the story.

Eventually, we reach the climax of the tale where she must make a Big Decision that will determine the outcome of the story, and that decision will pass a verdict on whether her original belief about compassion was correct after all or if a new one she's been developing the hard way over the course of the story is a truer fit. That could mean that the theme statement we *end* with, that is, her new belief on the theme, is something like this: truly compassionate people know how to say no. (This is a common theme and character arc for a Type 2 Helper protagonist.)

That change in her belief about the theme, that evolution, is the heart of our story.

That is why it is so important to nail down your theme statement. Maybe you start your draft knowing what your protagonist believes about the theme, or maybe you muddle your way through the draft and clean it up in revisions. Whatever your process is, it's fine. But if you can't articulate your protagonist's belief on the theme at the start and the finish of your story in a single sentence each, odds are high that readers will lack clarity on that as well and fail to gain the sense of meaning they're searching for.

That's why the theme statement is an important element. It helps the storyteller convey the meaning to the readers.

SERIES THEME

With what we've discussed with theme, you might be wondering how that plays out over the course of not just a book, but a series.

Just nod and say, "Sure, Claire, that's exactly what I was wondering." You'd arrive at the question eventually, at least.

The answer is that you establish a series theme. Not only is this a great way to differentiate your series in the mind of the reader once they've completed it, but it's also a great guide for *you* when you're a few books in and miserably moaning, "What the hell do I put in the next book?"

So, yes, each book will have a theme, but the series as a whole can also have an overarching theme. I'll explain how this works in a second, but first, let's talk about how you might decide on your theme on a book-by-book basis in a single series.

Your approach depends on a couple of things. First, *how* is this series a series? That is, what are the connecting factors? If we're talking a romance series, then generally each book will follow a different couple, meaning the books do not share a protagonist. In this case, the connective tissue of the series might be that all the stories take place in the same small town or within a single friend group. This gives you more room to skip from one theme to the next in each book and keeps things fairly simple in this sense. The only thing to watch out for is having two (or more) protagonists arrive at opposing beliefs on the same theme. Such a thing is likely to split your audience and could lead to a lot of one-star reviews.

If your series follows a single protagonist, then there is a little more to consider. For instance, jumping randomly from one theme to the next, book by book, may not be the strongest approach. It might be *fine.* For instance, the Robert Langdon series by Dan Brown tackles a fresh theme in each book with very little callback to the others, and I've heard his books are selling okay. However, Robert Langdon doesn't exactly grow as a character, and when we talk about Dan Brown, we're discussing the exception that proves the rule. No hate to him—I've enjoyed most of his books, think he's smart about storytelling, and he knows how to deliver a real page-turner—I just don't think the rest of us want to gamble by following his formula when stronger strategies exist.

So, yes, you can make your single-protagonist series one random theme after another, and those themes don't have to carry much coherence (or any at all) from book to book, and your protagonist can remain a bit of a stock character and a tour guide for the readers...

Or you can do something especially clever with theme in a series.

You can manage multiple themes.

How does this work when I've already told you to focus on a single theme for your book? Think of it in terms of thematic *overlays*. You develop your book's theme *within the context* of a larger series theme. Don't worry, I'll explain.

One of my favorite ways to write a series is what I've coined the Bookend Method. You establish a theme that is going to last for the duration of your series. You want to structure your series as you would structure a story, any story. You're going to take the basic structure that you would use in any book and expand it to a larger scale for your series. Your series should have an inciting incident, a fun midpoint turn, and a climax, essentially. The same storytelling wisdom applies.

Book one of your series will have its own inciting incident, midpoint, and climax. And what we usually see in strong series is that the climax of the first book serves as the inciting incident of the rest of the series. The protagonist's first Big Decision (climax of book 1) resolves the initial conflict but also results in a larger conflict that must be resolved in book two and beyond.

I suspect this is why I tend to like book two in any series less than all the rest, and maybe you feel the same. We're past the initial shock and awe of our protagonist leaving the ordinary world behind and entering into a new adventure, and now we find ourselves at the lowest point in the rising action of the *series*. Book twos tend to be a lot of setup, don't they? This is why. The book itself will have an inciting incident, etc., but in the grand scheme of the series, it's that point right after the inciting incident where something is off, but the protagonist isn't being incredibly useful about finding a solution yet.

Take, for instance, A Song of Ice and Fire (mild spoiler for book one, which you've had twenty-five years to read, so don't come at me). The first book, *A Game of Thrones*, is exciting because we're entering a whole new world. Everything is fresh and we're learning the rules. This Ned Stark guy seems solid, and we can't wait to see what he does in turning around the Seven Kingdoms once he goes down to—

Oh no.

Ned Stark is arguably the protagonist of the first book. His decisions drive the actions of the rest of his family, which makes sense because his children are still young and useless. It's also his decisions that lead to his beheading in the climax of the book.

Whoops! You chose poorly, Ned. You didn't adjust your initial beliefs to work in the world you live in, and now your story ends tragically.

Within the context of the first book, Ned's murder is the climax, but in the context of the series, it's the inciting incident. Nothing is the same afterward. It shakes up Westeros like nothing else. Villainy is exposed, new alliances are formed, and so forth. And the second book is arguably the least interesting one because it must be the setup for the rest of the series. Book three is... phew. Much more riveting. "The Rains of Castamere" starts playing, and shit gets real.

Now back to the Bookend Method and theme. It's structured the same way as our book-to-series-level plots that I just explained. In this method, each individual book should have its own theme. *And* the series itself should have a theme. So, what I like to do is double up on that series theme in the first and the last book of the series.

If my nine-book series has the theme of *equality*, book one will *also* have the theme of equality as its book-level theme, and book nine will revisit that same theme of equality at the book level.

"But if I do the same theme twice with the same protagonist—won't the books end up being the same?" Not if your protagonist has grown and changed over the course of books two through eight, which I sure hope they have. If that theme ends up presenting in the exact same way, then you probably have not developed your protagonist's inner world adequately. But that almost never happens, in part because *you* are not the same person when you write book one as when you write book nine. We transform and grow with our series, thankfully.

The fact is your protagonist can learn the same kind of lessons more than once. This is because *people* learn the same lessons more than once. We tend to learn things in broad strokes at first, and then slowly, through time and experience, we gain a more nuanced understanding of concepts like *equality*, or *courage*, or *worth*. Not to mention, there's the concept of self-forgetting we all experience, which is why we can move up and down the levels of development in the Enneagram. Sometimes we exhibit the healthy behaviors of our type, sometimes the average ones, and, on those rare and regretful occasions, the unhealthy ones. But the same lessons tend to pull us upward again and again.

The most important truths for our type to learn tend to be the hardest for us to remember. "Oh right," I say, for the thousandth time, "maybe I'm not a bad person because I made a harsh comment to my husband when I was hungry." One would think I'd learn after all these lessons life keeps handing me to accept that I am imperfect (and that's okay!), and yet...

Depending on your Enneagram type, there are going to be specific lessons you must learn again and again. Our core fear and desire blind us to realities that might seem obvious to other types. Those other types might not give very much consideration at all to the concepts that we spend our lives hung up on. Learning these important lessons for our type is not a one-and-done sort of thing, unfortunately. The themes we do battle with in our own lives can be clearly connected back to our core motivations. They are the hardest for us to learn and the most important, and because of that, we keep running up against them. The result, if we commit to the battles rather than avoid them, is that we eventually possess deep insight on those particular concepts, insight we can offer the world.

If you're a Type 6, and you're always confronting the same lesson about listening to your inner authority rather than seeking external authority to project you, you have the potential to gain deep insight on the concepts (i.e. themes) of authority, trust, and loyalty, whereas another type fighting different battles may lack the depth of insight due to focusing their energy on other recurring life themes.

The same holds true for your protagonist.

And that's why the Bookend Method works. Because your protagonist learns something important, gains some new insight or knowledge or growth regarding that important theme through the course of book one. Then that initial lesson informs the rest of the series, as it's tested again and again in different contexts until we return to it fully in the final book of the series. What we accomplish by returning to the initial theme is create a satisfying sense of closure for the reader. We close the loop, answer the lingering question, and pass the final verdict that supplies meaning. Humans like this. You see it in classical music all the time, when the piece returns to where it started and it feels like a sigh of relief. We like things to come full circle. When they don't, it can leave us uneasy. We may not even know we're uneasy; it's that subconscious. But we *do* know when we've read a truly satisfying ending. We put the book down and stare at the wall ahead of us and think, *I need to talk to someone about this.* That impulse is what creates word of mouth, which is, of course, the very best advertising you could hope for. Highest conversion rate around and entirely free.

The obvious next question is what do you do with the books in between the bookends, insofar as theme? I've used the phrase "within the context of" a few times so far, but I know that can be one of those annoying abstract phrases that seems like filler, that causes your eyes to glaze over a little bit and your brain to dismiss it as unimportant. Here's what I mean by it, though. Let's say your series theme is *belonging*. And let's say you have five books in your series. With the Bookend Method, you already know that the theme for books one and five will be *belonging*. What about books two through four?

You're free to pick different themes to explore.

Let's say your theme for book two in the series is *family*. At first blush, *family* may seem like one of those nouns, like Connecticut or baseball, that isn't really a theme. And if we're talking about your literal biological family, then there's an argument to be made that it's not a strong theme. But people mean all kinds of things when they talk about family. Imagine all the questions around what constitutes family, what role the people you call family play in decision making, and so on. Family is a fine theme.

So, for book two, you're going to be writing to the theme of family *in the context of* belonging, your series theme. That will raise questions like: What does it mean to *belong* in a *family*? What happens when you simply don't *belong* in your *family*? Can building your own *family* create a place where you *belong*? Do we *belong* more in our biological *family*, or our found *family*? When we must pick between those two, which one do we *belong* in?

If you're especially clever, your protagonist's theme statement will include both the book and series theme within it. Perhaps at the start of this hypothetical second book they believe that *family* is the only place where they truly *belong*. And because this is book two in the series, that belief is probably something that they learned or reaffirmed along the way in book one. But now we're challenging it. And over the course of book two, the protagonist's idea of belonging in family will change based on the events that challenge that existing idea, that theme statement, at the start.

Can you imagine what the inciting incident might be? Perhaps our protagonist discovers they're adopted. Or perhaps their family shuns them. Either one would make the belief that "family is the only place I truly belong" painfully untenable for the protagonist. Their emotional equilibrium would be upset, and they would immediately seek to reestablish solid ground.

This also means that a powerful climax for book two will address that specific belief about family and belonging. The decision your protagonist makes will be about that. This may seem constrictive, but what it's giving you is a clear philosophical and emotional roadmap for your book. If you like to plot your book ahead of time, you know what you're aiming toward in those beats. And if you like to pants it, no problem! You have a general idea of where you are headed in the climax with plenty of blank space for discovery along the way. If you get lost—not saying this is something that happens to pantsers *all the time*, and why I suggest at least jotting down a few notes for your outline—you know how to right the ship, what stars to align yourself by, and then you can continue pantsing away once again.

Onward. Book three of this five-book series about *belonging* might have a theme like *independence*. Ooh, *that's* challenging, isn't it? How does a sense of belonging interact with a human's need to be independent? Now we have some complex questions about group vs. individual that we get to explore. Can one belong to a group while maintaining genuine independence? How much independence is worth forfeiting to belong somewhere?

Then maybe the next book in the series, book four, has a theme of *responsibility*. What does responsibility look like in the context of belonging? Does belonging to a group take precedence over our responsibility to ourselves? What is our responsibility to those we belong with?

And after you explore that, in the final book, having learned what your protagonist has about family, independence, and responsibility, your protagonist will naturally possess more insight into the theme of belonging itself, some universal understanding of it that will help them make that final decision in the climax of book five that decides the outcome of the series.

If you've been paying very close attention, you might have noticed that you can grab just about any theme for those middle books in your series and it will interact in new and interesting ways with the series theme. This means you could have a hundred books in the series and each can feel fresh (assuming you don't want to walk into the woods and never return by book fifty or so).

What we're doing, in the most basic sense, is grabbing two data points: series theme and book theme. And as we and all conspiracy theorists know, you can draw a line between any two points. That's why this is an elegant solution to managing series and book themes without confusing ourselves along the way.

What do you do, though, if you don't know how many books are going to be in your series when you start out? I get this question a lot, and it's a great one because, let's face it, if you publish a few books in a series and it takes off in popularity and earns you exponentially more with each book launch, why in God's name would you put an end to it?

I mean, there are reasons. If you can't stand to write another word of it, you might consider at least taking a break. But let's say you're still enjoying it, and yes, you had an idea of how to end it after five books, but if you could get it to ten or even fifteen, you could probably retire in five years.

If you want to ride that book steed into the sunset, saddle up and do it! The Bookend Method allows for that, because once you know your series theme, you can keep adding book theme after book theme after book theme under that series theme, and it will continue to feel like a cohesive narrative. You will keep delivering more of the special ingredient that made readers love your series... because you'll know what it is!

Yes, that's right. Readers love certain genres and tropes, or at least that's what they think makes them fall deeply in love with a book or series, and sure, it plays a part. But it's the emotional connection to that deeper level of story that turns readers into superfans, and that's achieved through a strong and developed theme.

How many times have we seen "debut" authors soar to fame with their first book only to have the next one release to poor reception? In my research, I've found that this is often the result of the author developing a strong theme in the first book, then failing to develop one in the next. This can happen when we don't build our storytelling skill of theme development.

Can an author stumble upon a strong theme and pull it off without realizing that's what they're doing? Absolutely! It's rare, but it does happen, especially with the precious first book that the author could've been workshopping and developing for years.

When you account for the vast number of submissions to literary agents and publishers each year, it makes sense that a few of the books with accidentally developed themes would make the cut. It's a numbers game.

I say this to draw attention to not only the pitfalls of trying to skip over this skill, but to show how many authors have neglected it and how far ahead of the curve you will be with your storytelling skills if you give theme the attention and respect it deserves. Not only will you learn to write one amazing book, but your odds of the next one flopping are significantly lowered.

When you know your theme, you understand what you're delivering, and you can do it again and again to the benefit of your fans (and your pocketbook. I told you I don't hate money).

And then, someday in the distant future, when you finally reach the point where you either have enough money to live on for the rest of your life, or the later books in the series aren't making you enough to keep writing more, or you're simply sick of writing in this series and ready to move on, with the Bookend Method you only have to write one more book to give your series the satisfying ending that your loyal readers deserve.

You do that by revisiting the original theme, the book one theme that is also your series theme. Tie up all those loose plot ends and hit that final book and series climax hard with your protagonist passing a strong verdict on their original belief regarding the theme.

Sure, it might be a *very* long book if you've created a ton of loose plot threads and you decide spur the moment that this will be the last one, but you probably need only one more book-level narrative arc to provide your readers with a strong sense of emotional satisfaction, to leave them feeling like they didn't read all these books and grow attached to all your wonderful characters only to have it end on an emotional and philosophical cliffhanger.

Or worse, to have it end in an emotionally incoherent way.

And that's how you do it, folks! That's how you deliver not only a satisfying book but a satisfying series by using theme as the emotional and philosophical foundation of your story.

DECIDING ON YOUR THEME

With all of the options for your story's theme, how in the nine circles of hell do you settle on one?

Thankfully, there will be some that resonate with you more strongly because of your core fear and core desire. Yep. Some themes resonate with certain Enneagram types more than others, and this is great news for our author alignment process.

What gets your hackles up? What rules do you adhere to that irk you terribly when people violate them? If it sends you over the edge when you see people abuse their power, then maybe *power* is a theme that will interest you for at least the duration of a book if not a series. If double standards make you want to kick ass and take names, then maybe *equality* is a good theme for you to explore. Or *justice*. Or *fairness*.

"But Claire," you say, "*nobody* likes abuses of power or double standards."

Well, some people do or else those things wouldn't exist. But I understand your point, and it's a good one. Here's the thing, though: being *annoyed* and *fantasizing about murder* are different levels of irritation. Maybe you're not in the anger triad of the Enneagram (Eights, Nines, and Ones) like I am, but I do believe that everyone has a tipping point where the behavior of others slides past the line of basic annoyance into the territory of "This *fucking* guy..." and dreams of fisticuffs, even if you would never actually throw a punch. The particular behaviors that push you to the brink are great places to mine for the themes that hit deeply for you.

Additionally, we all have the concepts that we keep coming back to in our more introspective moments (our life themes) and stories that we tell ourselves about the world around us. When you're driving around with the radio off, what scenarios come to mind? (You're a writer with a big imagination, so I know this happens to you.) These could be fantasies about what you wish you'd said or imagined opportunities to do something grand. What is the conflict at the core of these scenarios?

Are you replaying a moment when the douchebag in line at Starbucks yelled at the barista and you said nothing, only now you're imagining yourself stepping in? (Core concept/theme: courage, justice, righteousness.)

Are you forecasting a possible rejection by a close friend or lover and trying to imagine a way you would go on afterward? (Core concept/theme: loneliness, belonging, rejection, connection.)

Because of the silly way the human brain is wired, we have an attention bias for the negative. That means we tend to stew over the things that left us with a bad taste in our mouth rather than savoring those moments that went perfectly for everyone involved. And when we turn our eyes to the future, we worry about the things that could go wrong (rather than right) in a misguided attempt to prepare for the hard parts of life. This is why I ask you to imagine the negative triggers to mine for themes; they naturally stand out to us more.

Once you know and begin to understand your Enneagram type, you can get real about what topics speak more to you than others. Why would we need to "get real" about this? Oh, I dunno, something about our culture and society force-feeding us what we "should" care about. But maybe, when you give yourself a little space to consider it, you'll realize that some of the strife you experience is from trying to care about things you could not actually care less about. What wasted energy!

This is what I mean. If you're a Type 2, the Helper, your driving desire to give help to others (in hopes of reaching a point where you're worthy of love) will naturally steer you toward themes like *responsibility*, *family*, and *belonging*. On the other side of that coin, you might also resonate with a theme of *rejection*.

Meanwhile, Type 5, the Investigator, is unlikely to be drawn to those same themes as strongly. Fives are in the head triad (Fives, Sixes, Sevens). It's sometimes said that Fives view their body only as the thing that moves their head around. They are firmly centered in the intellect. For that reason, they don't generally seek as much social connection as Twos, and when their thoughts wander to the topic of other people, it's more in a scientific sense than it is exploring the realm of emotion and interdependence. Ask a Five about sociology or psychology, and they might have that listed among their specific areas of study, but as far as themes go, something like *connection* is unlikely to hold their interests as long as it does a Two. Because Investigators' core fear and desire are about competency and self-sufficiency, themes like *truth* and *independence* are more likely to interest a Five instead.

This is yet another way that the self-knowledge we gain from the Enneagram can level up our writing. When we write to themes that excite and engage us, that passion helps us make it through the inevitably slow and sometimes excruciating parts of the creative process.

THEMES AND ENNEAGRAM

Here are some themes by type to get you started. But know that I'm hesitant to include it because I don't want it to be interpreted as exhaustive. It's not close to comprehensive, because that would be impossible, but take a look at your type and see if some of these themes are concepts that you think over frequently or feel strongly about. You'll notice that certain themes appear many times on the list, not just under one type. That's because no theme resonates solely with a single type. If only the Enneagram were that simple!

Type 1, the Reformer: justice, equality, imperfection, righteousness, belonging, goodness, evil, loneliness, responsibility, growth, acceptance (especially self-acceptance)

Type 2, the Helper: responsibility, connection, pride, family, love, worth, helping/enabling, identity, individualism, generosity, boundaries

Type 3, the Achiever: worth, happiness, contentment, success, support, vanity, status, connection, acceptance, significance

Type 4, the Individualist: purpose, identity, envy, loneliness, dependence, spirit, aspiration, dreams, addiction, obsession, significance, authenticity

Type 5, the Investigator: truth, reality, avarice, memory, loneliness, exploration, respect, independence, self-sufficiency, abundance/scarcity

Type 6, the Loyalist: loyalty, responsibility, trust, fear, authority, security, connection, abandonment, support, reliance, courage

Type 7, the Enthusiast: joy, pain, fear, avoidance, reality, contentment, responsibility, faith, satisfaction, freedom, abundance/scarcity

Type 8, the Challenger: courage, vulnerability, control, power, responsibility, destiny, conflict, significance, kindness, strength, leadership

Type 9, the Peacemaker: serenity, conflict, action, loneliness, connection/disconnection, avoidance, courage, responsibility, harmony, belonging, identity, significance

While these are themes that may resonate especially strongly with each dominant type, we don't *stay* in our dominant type all the time.

Under stress and in growth, we begin to resemble other types. This is part of what makes the Enneagram so versatile and so much more than a meme.

When we find ourselves under prolonged stress that is more than we can handle, one of our coping mechanisms to avoid dipping down into the unhealthy levels of our dominant type is to essentially hit the pressure release valve and pop over to our "stress type." And as we grow by untangling the patterns of our dominant type, we start to resemble the healthy version of our specific "growth type." Or, when we're feeling especially comfortable in a situation—around friends or family we trust, doing an activity that doesn't stress us out—we will resemble our growth type. This is called our "security type."

That's what the arrows in the diagram represent. Follow the direction of the arrow from any of the nine types, and you'll find the dominant type's growth/security type. Go in the opposite direction, and you'll find the dominant type's missing piece/stress type (we're absolutely not getting into the concept of missing pieces right now, don't worry).

Check it out and find your type's stress and growth numbers.

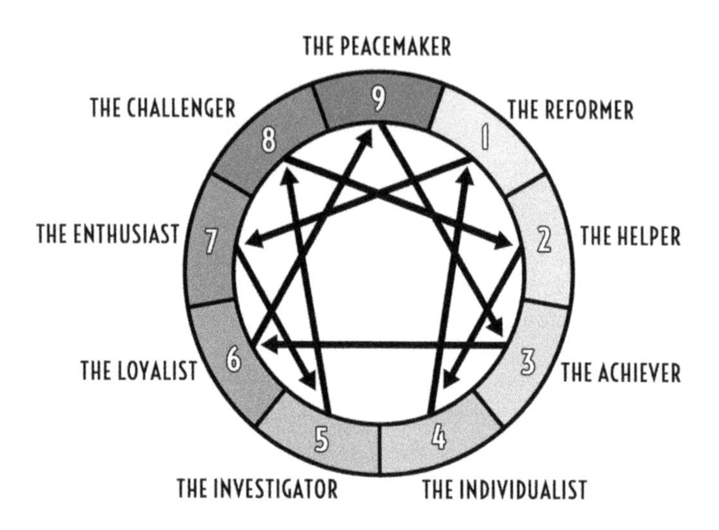

For clarification, look at Type 5. If you follow the arrow *away* from it, you end up at Type 8. Five goes to Eight in security and growth. If you follow the arrow pointing *to* Type 5 backward, you end up on Type 7. Five goes to Seven in stress.

Because of this possible movement between types, you don't need to limit yourself to the themes of your dominant type. It's just an easy place to start. For instance, if you're a Nine, you may have some interest in the words associated with the Six that you start to resemble in stress and the Three that you start to resemble in security.

You might also find some interesting themes that resonate with you in the One or Eight, since those are your wings. Most people tend to favor one wing over the other, so maybe you are more of a Five-wing-Six (written as 5w6) and the Six topics resonate with you. Or you're a 5w4 and the Four topics resonate with you.

Again, no need to confine yourself, but you might find it helpful to limit your initial search to your dominant type's listed themes. You'll know when you see one that looks exceptionally fun to write or that captures your interest immediately. Maybe you won't be able to stop thinking about it, or maybe it's already something that you haven't been able to stop considering recently.

Here's the thing: if you pick a topic that's aligned with your core motivations, then it's going to fall in line with your creative values and persona, which are aligned with the same thing: you. That's going to send a clear message to readers about what you offer. And so long as you stay consistent across your series within that single persona, your readers will come to trust you and trust that you will continually deliver something that resonates with them. They will know, to some degree, what to expect, no matter what genre you jump into or what media form your story takes. The economics of predictability should not be underestimated. Disney knows this. We ought to take heed.

By using themes aligned with you and who you are, it's easy to switch things up externally in your stories while maintaining the *essence* that readers love but can't quite put their finger on.

MANAGING MULTIPLE SERIES

If you have multiple series under a single persona or pen name—and I sincerely hope you do, because it can make you good money—what do you do about series theme? Must all of your series have the same theme? Definitely not. For one, by the time you finish up a series, you're probably out of gas on that series theme. At least for a little while. You've explored it in many ways from a variety of angles, and it may not be holding your interest like it once was. Totally fine! Grab a new theme for a new series!

There are all kinds of themes that will work for any given persona and that will interest you enough to make them worthy of exploring for the duration of a book series. No need to limit yourself to one.

It's important to note, though, that *similar* themes are a great way to make sure that your readers move from one series to the next. It can be crazy hard to convert readers from one series to even a spin-off series with many of the same characters. If you pick a drastically different theme for your next series, you'll likely lose even more people. So, going from a theme of *courage* to a theme of *sacrifice* is a comfortable lateral step. The protagonist of each of these series will likely be asked to make many of the same types of decisions, and they might find themselves in similar emotional situations that could look vastly different in the external world. It takes a lot of *courage* to embody *sacrifice*, just like it often takes a willingness to *sacrifice* to show *courage*. If you're writing something like epic fantasy, these two themes will feel familiar to the seasoned epic fantasy reader without feeling entirely redundant.

But if you make a leap from series to series that takes readers from a theme of *love* to a theme of *grief*, you risk a mass exodus of readers. The tone between series is likely to vary dramatically, and readers who came for the oxytocin that you provided through the theme of *love* might not be up for the gut-wrenching scenes or cathartic cry that you're delivering with the tale about *grief*.

So considering the emotional coherence between your series themes as you move from one to the next does you and your readers a huge favor. And if you absolutely need to take a hard turn toward a different kind of theme—say your heart is pulling you in that direction and you don't think you can move forward until you address this particular story—that's fine, too. You can do that. I give you permission if you need it. But it's important to adjust your expectations. Don't expect every reader to board the ride if you're taking that hard turn. Perhaps many will if you prime them through your communications and spin them a yarn about why that story means so much to you. Maybe even give them a way to be notified when you go back to the way things were, and then do what you gotta do. Fulfill that writing motivation, just don't feel entitled to making same the kind of money you might have if you'd stuck with the economics of predictability.

WHAT IS YOUR STORY ABOUT?

Theme doesn't have to be complicated or confusing, despite how I felt in my college classes. In fact, the whole purpose of it is to clarify and simplify the heart of your story. It doesn't get much simpler than a single word, when you think about it.

You'll inevitably come across other definitions of "theme" as you navigate the writing space, but I'm here to tell you: you have permission to ignore them if this one makes sense to you. It's plenty to build a book or even a series on without getting tripped up.

So, next time someone asks you what your story is about, what are you going to say?

HOMEWORK

1. What are three themes (concepts) you've been doing battle with lately in your life?
2. Pick one of the three that resonates strongly with you. List five different views/beliefs someone could have about that word.
3. How do you think your current and/or ideal readers would resonate with this theme?

CHAPTER 6
WHO ARE MY PROTAGONISTS?

MEET YOUR PROTAGONIST

In this chapter we're diving deeper into the story by talking all about your protagonist.

A story is about characters, and the protagonist is the character whose actions determine what the story is *about*. So, mastering the art of the protagonist is important to your career.

Let's take a quick look at the concentric circles again. Protagonist is at the center, so you want to make sure you pick the right someone to be at the center of each story, someone who makes sense with your creative values, persona, and the story's theme.

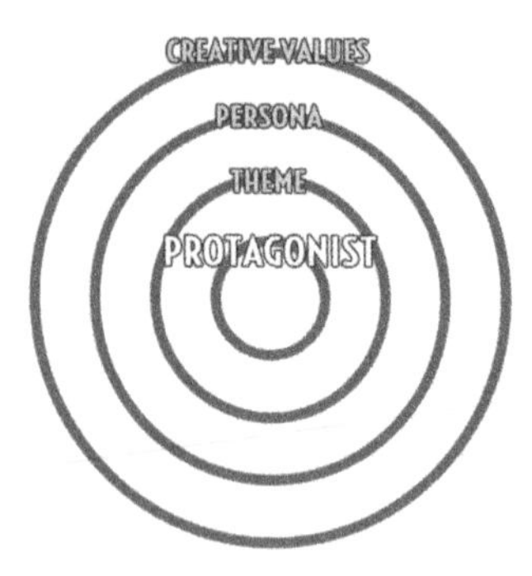

But if we're going to create coherent and aligned stories, you can't talk about the protagonist without also talking in depth about the theme. The journey of your protagonist is inextricably connected with the theme, as we discussed in the last chapter.

So, have you decided on a theme for your next story? Or maybe you have it narrowed down to two or three that you might want to write about. That's fine. No need to decide on one just yet.

You probably have a strong *personal* theme statement for each of your possible themes, but that doesn't mean that your protagonist's feelings on the topics must, or should, match, especially at the start of the story. Your protagonist can hold a different belief from yours in the exposition then come around to your way of thinking by the resolution. Or they can think something different and *never* come around to your way of thinking. Or *your* way of thinking can change as you explore the theme through the confines of your story. All kinds of wonderful things can happen! But it's important to get clear on how your beliefs may differ from your protagonist's in important ways.

THE THREE CENTERS

One thing you want to make sure of is that you understand *how* your protagonist and theme interact. And the key to that is understanding who your protagonist is. I'm not talking what sport they played as a kid, where they live, or a traumatic childhood memory, though you can certainly figure those things out in your process to add color and depth.

Obviously, I'm talking about their Enneagram type. Because to know your protagonist, you need to know their core motivations. What do they fear and what do they desire? What repels them and what draws them forward?

You can pick any of the nine types for your protagonist and that's A-OK. There's no wrong answer. But there are some pairings of type to theme that are naturally stronger than others, as we discussed in the theme section.

The way we experience the world varies from type to type, but there are also these groupings within the Enneagram called "triads." They're each comprised of three types that share an important similarity, and the one I want to focus on here is the head, heart, and gut triads (also called the thinking, feeling, and instinctive triads).

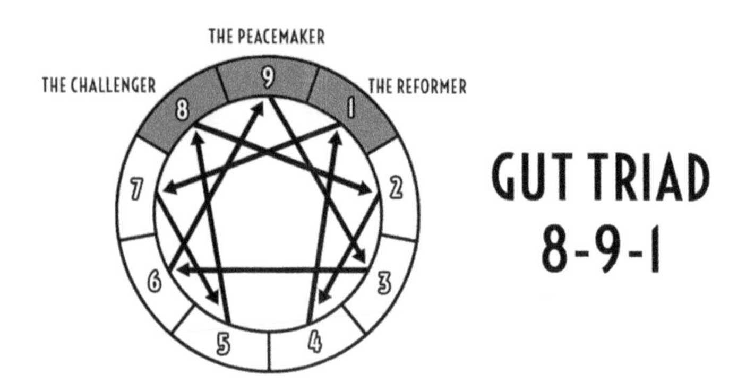

Folks who are one of these types experience the world through their body first. Sometimes called the instinctual triad, their body alerts them to information before their rational thinking and emotions can catch up. They just *know* something's off and then have to pause to put the clues together. People in this triad function on their "gut" instinct, sometimes called intuition.

Eights (Challengers) often forget to take the time to intellectualize and understand the gut instincts before acting on them. They can charge in headlong before thinking things through. At the same time, they're often the first to speak up at injustice and attempt to neutralize a threat, since they don't have to intellectualize the injustice to validate their action on it or wade through emotions before proceeding. Straight into action, Eights.

Nines (Peacemakers) often dismiss the gut feelings and bury them down deep or mistrust them. But as Nines move into healthier levels, they use their natural intuition to read the room in an effort to maintain group cohesion. The anger associated with this triad that Eights express so easily causes Nines to disconnect from their gut to avoid the disruption of inner and outer peace that the anger energy can lead to. Yet it's still there. If they're not mindful, Nines express it through passive-aggression and stubbornness. Usually, though, the peaceful energy of a Nine is unmistakable when you're in its presence.

Ones (Reformers) often try to intellectualize their gut instincts too quickly, desperate to restore emotional and mental equilibrium. Ones get a read on people and situations in the blink of an eye, make no mistake, but they won't always let on. Because Ones are desperate not to do or say the wrong thing, they tend to hold everything inside until they can weigh the options on their imaginary scales of right and wrong then decide how best to react. When Ones are living at healthy levels, they are tapped into their well of intuition and possess instant decision-making skills, guided by their body's responses.

Each of these types experiences emotions in a *visceral* way. The gut triad is also known as the anger triad. Challengers get aggressive, Peacemakers get passive-aggressive, and Reformers show few signs of it until it comes out in weird bursts, frequently as a desire to punish.

The important thing to remember when you're writing gut triad protagonists is that they experience the world through their body first. Lean into their intuition.

Folks of these types are emotion-based individuals. Emotions hit hard initially (unless they're the disconnected Three), then the person can either rationalize them away or feel their way through, but only after the initial collision.

Twos (Helpers) often downplay or reject their emotions so they don't burden others with them. Twos have an amazing ability to tap into the emotions of others to figure out how best to serve their needs. But ask a Two what they themselves need, and you might leave them wide-eyed and confused. When you determine your worthiness of love by what you can give, the emotions behind accepting help can be turbulent, to say the least. In this way, they often tap into the emotions of others while neglecting their own emotions. But those emotions don't go away.

Threes (Achievers) are by nature out of touch with their emotions, but they still experience the world that way first, and it can cause an unpleasant disconnect that must be resolved. Similarly to Twos, Threes are good at reading the emotions of others, though they use that ability for slightly different purposes. Threes figure out who others *want* them to be (as opposed to Twos, who figure out what others *need* from them), and then they have an uncanny ability to suppress their own emotions to become the person others consider valuable. And yet no matter how much Threes reject their emotional base in service to their goals, it's always there. Ignore it long enough, and there's a train wreck looming.

Fours (Individualists) tend toward overidentifying with and overindulgence of emotions, failing to turn them into anything productive. They don't focus so much on the emotions of others, as the Twos and Threes do, getting lost in their own feelings instead. The biggest obstacle for Fours is that they tend to anchor their sense of identity to their emotions, and because emotions constantly ebb and flow, Fours can struggle with defining a personal identity for themselves. That in turn can lead to a fixation on the question of "Who am I?" that lasts a lifetime if not addressed.

The heart triad is also the shame triad. Helpers internalize the shame of having emotions (and needs), Achievers try to avoid it through stoic accomplishments, and Individualists often overindulge in the shame. When writing a heart triad protagonist, keep in mind that they will feel emotions associated with a situation first, even if they become so talented at rejecting those emotions that they lose conscious contact with them. Shame will keep these characters from doing many of the things they need to do for a healthy life, and you, the author, can use that as a reason why they cause problems for themselves.

For folks in the head triad, they experience the world through their minds first. This can take the form of data collection. These types are primarily functioning from an intellectual base, which looks different for each type.

Fives (Investigators) have little interest in or access to their emotions or intuition, often to their own detriment. Of all the types, Fives might be the most trapped within their own triad, and it can be a big challenge for them to tap into their body sensation or emotions. But that doesn't mean they don't have either of those things—it just means their task is to reconnect with them, and in the end, that will expand their knowledge of the world.

Sixes (Loyalists) use their mind to predict possible future problems. They can develop a strong gut instinct, but only after a ton of growth work. Their struggle is to connect to their inner authority, but being in the fear triad makes that tricky. Instead, they turn to data collection and mental games of worst-case-scenario thinking. Making decisions can be excruciating for Loyalists because they fall victim to decision by committee, the committee being all the voices in their head. Only once they develop trust of their intuition can they free themselves from the endless "what-ifs" that keep them anxious.

Sevens (Enthusiasts) tend to escape too much thinking and avoid spending much time in their head. In that way their intellect becomes their dictator, just as the rebellious teen is still acting in relation to their parents when they rebel rather than acting independently, as they might tell themselves they are. Activity, distraction, and novel stimulation are the Seven's way of avoiding the ugly thoughts as well as the ugly emotions and sensations that are an unavoidable part of life. Because of this, they tend to tap into their body for distractions from any unpleasant thoughts and emotions.

The head triad is also the fear triad. Investigators escape the fear by locking themselves away and pursuing safe areas of interest, Loyalists are always either moving toward or away from fear (either way, it's dictating much of what they do), and Enthusiasts prefer to avoid the fear by staying busy and experiencing new things.

When you're writing a protagonist in the head triad, be sure to consider how they intellectualize the world, and show that as much as possible.

If you find yourself writing across the triads, meaning your personal dominant type is in one and your protagonist's is in another, you're going to have to pay close attention to keep from blurring the types. We are so entrenched in our own way of experiencing the world—through emotions, intellect, or our body first—that we don't notice we're doing it. "What's water?" asks the fish.

That doesn't mean it's a deal breaker to write a protagonist across triads. Not by any stretch. But as with everything related to the Enneagram, the first step to unlocking is noticing. We must recognize that there are differences and what those differences are before we can crack the code to write a cohesive character that isn't a mishmash of our type and another.

Writing across triads can be *hard*. Think about how you describe the world. Is your protagonist experiencing it the way you do, or the way they *would* based on what triad they fall under and the unique lens of their type?

And even if you're writing within your same triad but writing a different number from yours, there are smaller differences to consider.

If you're a Seven (Enthusiast), say, and you're writing a Six (Loyalist) protagonist, both are in the head triad. But when money gets tight, you might laugh it off and distract yourself from the problem (a typical Seven response) and make lavish dinner plans with friends to avoid the fear of being broke and deprived. That's not likely the response of a Loyalist. Yes, they are still making their decisions in relation to the issue, but if they're a phobic Six, they're very likely going to lock down all their accounts and not spend a dime until they can find a way to get more money in. They will not be joining you at the expensive restaurant.

What I suggest, to avoid these complications, is to write a protagonist who's the same type as you. It's a simple trick, but a damn useful one. Align those core motivations.

Trust me, I've tried to write protagonists that were a different type. It's *so much trickier* to maintain coherence, and there's really no need to try.

Once you start to understand the Enneagram and master what the types look and act like, you're welcome to venture out and take the risk of writing a protagonist of a different type if you're up for the challenge. I suggest making it a type you're well familiar with, though, like your security or stress type or the type of your partner whom you see and interact with every day.

But first, why not just stick to your own type? You already know it will be aligned with 1) your creative values, 2) your persona, and 3) your theme. And you'll know exactly how all those elements interact.

We're all about saving energy here, and this is one of the fastest ways to do that.

ALIGNING WITH THEME

You want to make sure that your protagonist resonates with your theme. By aligning both to your type, you can pretty much ensure this, since you picked a theme based on what resonated with you.

That doesn't mean you should make your protagonist an exact avatar for you. After all, they'll likely have a drastically different personal history, which will shape them in specific and unique ways.

But when you stop and ask yourself, "How would these events shape her?" you'll have a much easier time figuring it out when you share those same core motivations.

For example, if you and your protagonist are both Type 6, the Loyalist, you're going to crave security and support. Let's say you, the author, were raised by two loving parents that made you feel secure and cared for and gave you the skills you needed to leave the nest and feel like you could keep yourself safe and secure in adulthood. Great! (I don't know how you became a writer with the perfect upbringing, but I digress.)

Now, let's say your protagonist *didn't* have all those things—maybe he didn't know his parents, or he was raised by an alcoholic father who didn't protect him or make him feel secure, and maybe this all takes place on a pirate ship.

The circumstances aren't anything like what you, a landlubber with stable parents, have experienced, but you can put yourself in there and say, "How would *I* feel about this?" and (major cultural differences aside) you could come up with a pretty close guess because you have the same triggers around security and support as your protagonist. But if your protagonist has *different* triggers, say if they're a Type 4 (the Individualist) and more concerned with understanding their place in the universe than worrying about their physical and social safety, then you can't just stick yourself in there and trust that the resulting picture will be accurate. The two of you are looking at the world through entirely different lenses.

Think about this: how many times has a good friend come to you distraught and told you what happened, but you just don't understand *why* they were so upset?

This is a prime example of different core triggers at play. "My girlfriend says she wants to get married" might be a negative trigger for your friend who's a Seven (the Enthusiast) and is afraid of anything that might restrict their freedom and independence. But if you're a Six (the Loyalist), the prospect of marriage *might* sound real frickin' nice. Attaching yourself to someone you love for life? Knowing there will always be someone there to comfort you in your hard times? Bring it on! (Of course, as the wedding day approaches, that Six-ness might manifest in a *lot* of anxiety and worst-case thinking, but that's for a later date.)

This is just one example, but hopefully you're starting to see why aligning core motivations, and the accompanying emotional triggers, with your protagonist could save you a major headache down the line.

THE THREE TYPES OF CONFLICT

In this section, I'll reveal the trick for building a satisfying ending to every book you write. Sound good? Cool.

You might be wondering which you should decide on first: your theme or your protagonist.

Either one is fine. Whichever one strikes inspiration for the story you want to tell is the one to start with. Sometimes you'll have to think of the right protagonist to help you explore a theme, and sometimes you'll have to think of the right theme to challenge your desired protagonist.

Once you have an idea of these two things—protagonist and theme—it's time to decide what strong belief your protagonist holds about the theme at the very start of the story, that is, the theme statement that we discussed in the last chapter. As a reminder, this belief is flawed in some way—too unrefined, faulty, or just plain harmful—and your protagonist may or may not be aware that they hold it.

Let's walk through how changing your protagonist's type can drastically change what the story is about.

Say your protagonist is a Seven (Enthusiast) and the theme you've chosen is *freedom*. Her theme statement at the start could be: "Freedom is more important than security." This is a common belief, right? But it's also a debatable one, and stated in fairly black-and-white terms. It could use closer examination and refinement at the very least, because where do you draw the line, right? Americans have been debating this in almost every arena since the 9/11 terrorist attacks.

The inciting incident of the story needs to challenge this belief. That's easy enough. She sees someone use their freedom to cause harm to someone she cares for deeply. Suddenly, we're out of the realm of theoretical and taking that theme statement into a personal and practical place. And it doesn't feel right anymore. She doesn't feel like the aggressor or people like him should continue to have the freedom to cause this level of pain. But where does that leave her belief on freedom? Uh-oh!

She can't continue to hold on to that theme statement in the way she believed it before. Everything's changed now. Her solid ground of belief has crumbled, and now her focus is on restoring her footing. There's our story. The protagonist becomes disconnected from themself as their belief is upended, and now they're on a quest to reconnect.

Just by picking an Enneagram type and a theme, I was able to come up with an inciting incident on the fly, because that pairing lends itself to certain kinds of conflict. Now think about if I'd chosen a Six (Loyalist) instead of the Seven (Enthusiast)?

The theme statement about freedom probably would have been something like this: "Freedom is a threat to personal security." Now, the inciting incident will probably be a moment when the protagonist, in trying to keep a loved one safe, causes that person to abandon them forever for a little breath of fresh air. Maybe our protagonist's sheltered child moves to the other side of the world upon graduation and ends up hurt because they were reacting to the protagonist's overbearing restriction by being reckless. Suddenly, in trying to protect, the Loyalist realizes they've done their child a disservice by not allowing enough freedom prior to graduation. They can't go back to their old belief about freedom now. And so, the rising action begins...

Frankly, I don't think a Loyalist is *as* strong of a pairing with *freedom* as an Enthusiast. But a Loyalist would make an excellent *antagonist* for an Enthusiast struggling with the theme statement of "Freedom is more important than security." They would provide an incredible philosophical counterpoint.

Your rising action will continue to challenge your protagonist's changing or stubbornly unchanging belief about the theme at every turn through a strong counterargument from the antagonist and the events and environments that test the protagonist's commitment to their initial (mis)belief.

It all builds up to the climax. That's the deciding moment where your protagonist makes a choice directly related to the theme. So, this is kinda important.

The theme statement is a philosophical claim at its heart. It is the foundation of the philosophical conflict of the story. But there are three types of conflict in any story: philosophical, emotional, and physical.

The external conflict is made up of the physical conflict—the movements and actions that happen in physical space outside the characters' minds.

The internal conflict is made up of two things. First, there's the emotional conflict, which is how the protagonist *feels* about the situation they're in. We all know what it feels like to be emotionally conflicted. This is the love triangle, the wanting to stay but feeling like you should leave. Emotional conflicts arise when the easy thing and the right thing are not the same thing, when we know what would be best for others but it takes something from us to follow through on that with action.

The second half of the internal conflict is the philosophical conflict, which relates back to the protagonist's belief about the theme. This is the tension that follows a belief being upended. Where do we stand now?

Imagine that your Type 1 (Reformer) protagonist believes that God rewards people who do the right thing (religious beliefs usually fall under the header of "philosophical"). Maybe they grew up in a religious family and believed that evangelizing was the right thing to do, and within their community they were revered for their zeal.

And then they go on a mission trip. Maybe evangelizing amidst poverty earns them no praise and no longer feels like the right thing to do amongst all the suffering. They might begin to refine their definition of "reward" and "right thing" in their theme statement, and the seeking of this new understanding is the heart of the story.

Here's a popular example of how the three types of conflict work together that is spoiler-y, but it's Harry Potter, so you've had your chance to read it:

The *physical* conflict of the last Harry Potter book is the Battle of Hogwarts. The question is: *Who will win?*

The *emotional* conflict is how Harry feels about what he must do to beat Voldemort. The question is: *Will he sacrifice himself for the greater good?*

And the philosophical conflict is all about the theme of the books: love. So the question is: *Will the selfless love that Harry's mother showed him be enough to defeat evil?* More succinctly: *Can love defeat hate*?

Those are the questions we, the readers, want answers to, whether we're aware of it or not. If those questions weren't answered, we would feel incredibly unsatisfied, even if we couldn't articulate why.

As a writer, you want to pose these kinds of questions toward the beginning of your story and then answer them in as short of a timespan as possible at the climax of your story. The closer together we get these answers, the better. If you can answer all of them in a single action by your protagonist, you've just delivered a killer ending.

J. K. Rowling does a solid job by answering the questions that have been building over seven books in a matter of about two chapters, and these questions are answered through the actions and reasoning of the protagonist (Harry).

This is why it's so important to know how your protagonist and theme determine the story you're telling. If you understand both pieces on their emotional and philosophical levels, you more or less know what your climax will need to look like. It will need to answer the philosophical question created by the disruption of your protagonist's theme statement in the inciting incident. You can read that a second time, and I wouldn't blame you. I just told you the key to knowing how to end every story in a satisfying way.

ALIGNING WITH PERSONA

When talking about theme statement and alignment, it's important to note that the protagonist's beliefs on the theme at the start of the book probably will not align with your beliefs that you express through your persona. This is partly a practical matter, since it helps to be a few steps ahead of your protagonist if you're going to be the captain of the ship.

So, if your protagonist's initial belief contradicts one of your own, readers aren't going to care, because readers *expect* to see a change. However, on the other side of that climax, your protagonist is probably going to have a fresh belief on the theme. And it's best if that belief aligns with the persona you've created and your creative values. (It automatically aligns with your theme, because it's *about* the theme, so you don't have to worry about that.) The message you're sending to your readers via your protagonist will feel like a betrayal if it runs counter to the messaging you're sending through your persona/brand.

Imagine if one of the things you highlighted in your persona was your blissful marriage. Maybe you write cute and funny stories about you and your husband in your newsletter or post them on social media. You draw your readers in with this idea of a healthy marriage. Fantastic! So glad that's working out for you! Now, if all your books are about marriage betrayal, or how marriage is a sophisticated form of female servitude, that's what I might call a misalignment, and not exactly a subtle one.

And same goes for your creative values. Don't make the protagonist pass a verdict you don't personally agree with to a large extent (*unless* you're writing a tragedy and want to show how this flawed belief leads to misery). That may seem like it goes without saying, and I wish it did. The truth is that sometimes we will ask our protagonists to pass down a verdict that we think that kind of character in that kind of genre *should* pass down. We forget to ask ourselves if we believe there's any truth to it. Just because you may be writing a protagonist with a different Enneagram type from your own doesn't mean that you can't mostly agree on the decision they make in the climax and the beliefs they hold at the conclusion of your story.

For instance, if you don't believe in monogamy, it might be a stretch to write monogamous romance with HEAs. So, maybe consider writing happy-for-nows instead. Or write menage/reverse harem instead. Over time, the misalignment between what you and your protagonists believe *will* make you fall out of love with your stories. Maybe you can knock out a few books this way, but misalignment always costs something, and it's a cumulative expense.

That's not to say your beliefs can't evolve along with your protagonist's! This wonderful surprise can be some of the most fulfilling writing there is. Perhaps you've just experienced one of *your* beliefs being upended, but you don't know how to adjust it yet. And so you write a story about a protagonist who just experienced the same philosophical upending, and through the proxy of your protagonist, you explore the topic. You stress-test possible replacement beliefs through your main character. And then eventually, you and your protagonist arrive at something new that works and restores equilibrium to your life as well as theirs. Phew! What a *personal* book to write, huh?

Maybe later on, you realize that the belief you and your protagonist arrived at was in itself flawed! Not a problem. This happens all the time (it's why growth work takes for-fucking-ever). And now you have fodder for another book.

MULTIPLE PROTAGONISTS

What happens if you have multiple protagonists? How do you align that?

Let me first explain what I mean by "multiple protagonists" and what I don't mean.

Here's what I don't mean: two protagonists in the same book. Trying this is unlikely to work out well for you. Now that you understand the protagonist's narrative purpose, insofar as providing structure to your story on the philosophical and emotional levels, you might already understand why you want to stick to just one per book.

Yes, even in a romance, there is only one protagonist. Assuming you have a romance involving two people, one will be your protagonist, and the other will function as the antagonist. This works because "antagonist" and "villain" aren't perfectly synonymous. Your antagonist *can* be villainous, but all they *must* be is a philosophical counterweight to your protagonist.

It is damn near impossible to have two people experience an epiphany and pass a verdict at the exact same time, which is why there is only one protagonist. If you read a lot of romance, think back on the books you've read recently and you'll start to see this dynamic emerge. Both characters need to grow and change, yes, but one of them will be the ultimate gatekeeper to the romance, the one to say "yes" or "no," and their decision will determine the fate of the pairing.

Incidentally, this is also how you would want to structure a buddy cop story. It's how I structured my Kilhaven Police series, making the rookie cop the protagonist and his field training officer the antagonist. They're technically working toward the same goal, but she (the FTO) is the force he (the rookie) must confront to pass his boards and reach full employment with the department in book one. She continues to present the main challenge to his philosophical views throughout the rest of the series.

So, when I'm talking about multiple protagonists, I'm talking over the course of a *series*. This is totally possible to do without digging yourself into a deep hole of narrative confusion, and when you have multiple protagonists over the course of a series (one per book), the strength of your theme becomes especially important to unite those books so they feel more like a single series rather than a series of random books stuck together.

What you want to do if you have a series with multiple protagonists is to unite them with the series theme (the book-level themes can vary, so don't worry too much about that).

Do all the protagonists need to share your Enneagram type to remain aligned? No, but this is where you will do yourself a huge favor by learning a little about each of the types so that you can write them.

In this case, despite my previous warning, I suggest you pick protagonist types different from your own. Now that you understand more about the possible pitfalls of this, you know to keep an eye out, especially at the big decision points, to make sure you're letting your protagonist react and decide as *they* would, not as *you* would in those situations. Be sure it makes sense for them to be stressed when they are, rather than stressed when you would be. It's a challenge, but that makes it stimulating!

However, even with protagonists of multiple types, my suggestion that their verdict align with your persona and creative values still stands. There can be exceptions to this, of course, but until you master this part, we're not going to get into the exceptions. Those work on more of a case-by-case basis and would be a more appropriate discussion for one of my author alignment calls.

Whether your protagonist is the same type as you or a different one, they are the main vehicle for your story. Their core desire is the gas pedal, and their core fear is the brake. Understanding them is how you remain in the driver's seat and ensure you enjoy the ride.

HOMEWORK

1. What Enneagram type will your protagonist be?
2. What is your protagonist's theme statement at the start of the story (prior to the inciting incident)?
3. What will/might be their verdict in the climax?
4. What part of you, the author, can be found in the protagonist? Do you share the same core triggers, a few qualities, non-core fears? And if so, what are they?

CHAPTER 7
BRINGING IT TOGETHER

YOUR INDIE AUTHOR CAREER

I hope the ideas we've discussed are assembling themselves into some kind of defined shape for you. These are big ideas, practically a whole new mindset from what most folks in the industry are teaching. These chapters don't contain a bunch of cute writing tips but rather a whole career philosophy. That's why you're here, though, right? You're ready to shuck what no longer serves you in this business and supercharge your gifts.

The goal for this chapter is to reinforce how each of the four elements of your author career interact so you know how to make the right decisions for your writing and marketing by knowing what questions to ask and when.

Let's start by returning to the concentric circles, now that we have a better understanding of each:

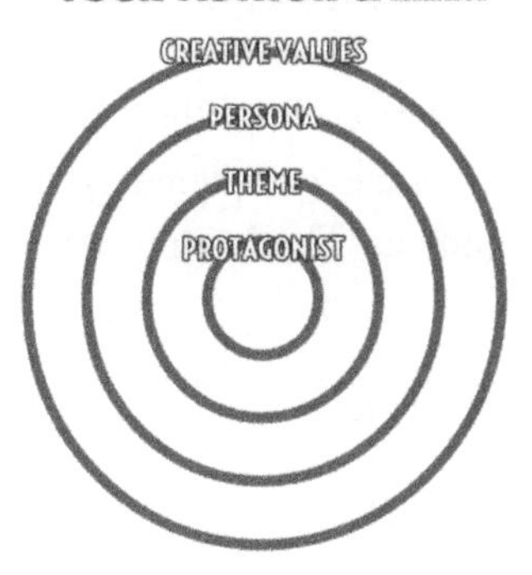

This representation only covers one series with a single protagonist. But you're likely going to write many series in your lifetime, each with a new protagonist or multiple protagonists, if you're writing something like romance.

Over the span of your career, then, it may start to look more like this:

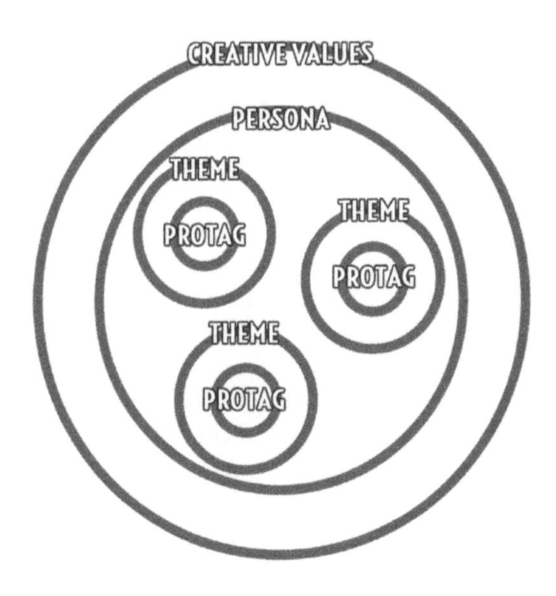

The concentric circles of your creative values and persona are still the same, but within those two circles are three smaller theme circles, and within each of those a smaller protagonist circle. Every smaller circle complements the circles encompassing it. That's alignment. That's our goal here.

TEN YEARS LATER...

I want you to imagine your body of work ten years from now. Maybe you're a writer that puts out a dozen books a year, or maybe one a year makes more sense for you. Either way, your catalogue will not be insubstantial ten years from now. And the odds of you holding the exact same views and priorities then as you do now are small. At least that's the hope, right? We hope to keep growing and changing over the course of our lifetime. Positive personal evolution is a thing to revere, not fear.

Will growth make our writing inconsistent over time? Not at all, so long as we anchor ourselves in the things that don't change about us: our core motivations.

That's right. Enneagram experts agree—you stay the same dominant type your whole life. That's yet another reason why it's such an amazing anchor for your career. The Enneagram framework is *built* for growth. It shows us a roadmap for our growth based on our type. But the core fears and desires stay the same. We simply learn to interact with them in more conscious and healthy ways.

By anchoring yourself in your core creative values, you clear out room to grow and change in a way that allows readers who love you at the start of your career to continue to resonate with your work decades later. Because your persona has attracted the right people for who you are deep down, those people will want to take the journey with you through your life as you produce different meaningful works. The stories will grow with you, and that's as it should be. Meanwhile, all of your works will contain that intangible element that readers fall in love with but can never quite put their finger on: you.

AUTHOR OF A THOUSAND FACES

What if you have multiple pen names, hence multiple personas, throughout your career? How does that affect this alignment thing?

Listen, I get it. I've had five pen names since going indie. First of all, I *don't* recommend having that many. It's exhausting because each one is its own business venture. I now advise authors to consider creating a new pen name *only* if they have a damn good reason to (I learn from my mistakes, which is the most I can hope for with how many mistakes I make).

But if you absolutely need to create a new pen name, that is, if you're sure the audiences you'll be writing for are so vastly different that by launching your new series under your existing pen name, you'll drive away your existing readers in droves (or create overwhelming brand confusion), we can work with that.

You'll need a new persona, but the rules still apply. Make sure your persona is an authentic slice of you, and align your series themes and protagonists with that particular slice.

The circles might then look like this:

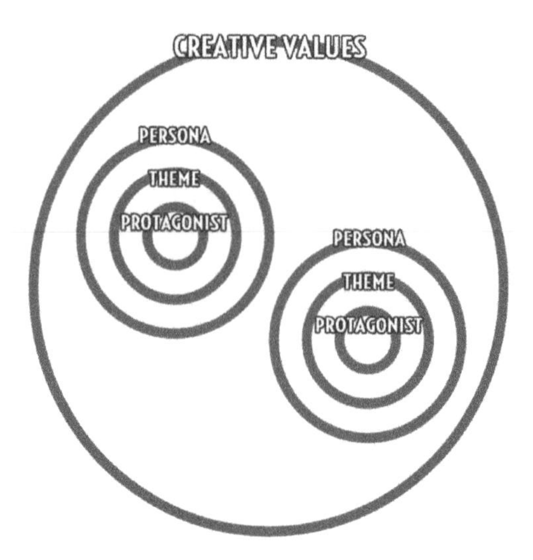

This time, only the creative values circle remains the same size, and within it are two smaller persona circles, with concentric theme and protagonist circles inside each. Or, if you prefer for it to look a little less nipple-y, here's another way to think about it:

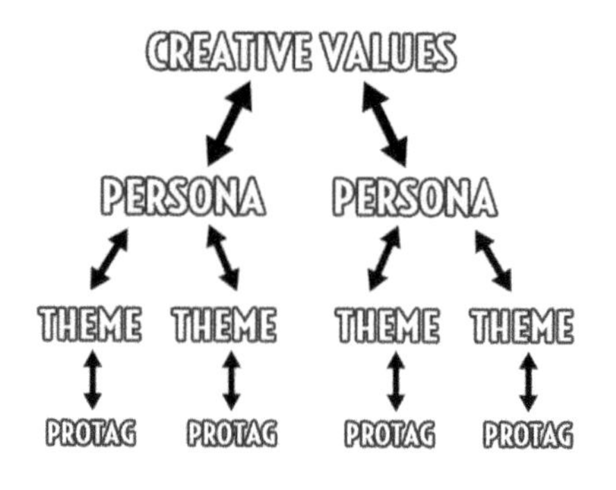

In this flow chart, when you pick a single end point of the chart, you should be able to trace it all the way back up to the top and have each element fall into alignment with the ones before it. And it's totally possible to do that with the framework I've described in this book!

AN EXAMPLE CAREER

So now that we have a clearer idea of how all these components build on each other, let's look at some hypothetical examples for each type. Let's build out an author's career from the outermost circle in.

EXAMPLE TYPE 1 CAREER

Creative Values: Ones are focused on being good and having integrity and avoiding becoming evil or corrupted, since those are their core motivations. This can lead to perfectionism as much as it can to impressive integrity. Ones also tend to care a lot about quality. This is not what others consider quality; it's what the *One* considers quality. Assuming the standards aren't being completely run by impossible-to-achieve perfectionism (which is sometimes the case), it's important for a One to respect this need in their process.

The natural desire for Ones to "fix" what they believe to be broken often forms itself into a sort of life mission. It's why they're called Reformers. They want to make the world a better place, and this mission is almost always the main source of fuel for their writing.

How this translates to career strategy is that a One might be able to grit her teeth and rapid-release books for a while on sheer puritanical work ethic, but if she is releasing books that don't meet her basic quality standards for the sake of speed, she is heading for disaster. Like, fifty-car-pile-up-type disaster. So, knowing full well that her goal of high-caliber work that supports her mission can easily slip into perfectionism, this One remains mindful of this inner tension without forcing herself to sacrifice her standards for the sake of speed.

It's not unusual for a One to believe that if she starts a secret pen name, she'll escape her internal quality standards and be able to achieve a faster publishing speed. This might work to churn out a few books quickly, but once the secret pen name gains a following, those standards come crashing back. This it because that need for quality is *internal* rather and *external*. There is no pen name she can create that keeps her separate from herself. So this One has decided to respect her comfortable publishing speed and enjoy the fruits of high-quality books, though the fruit may take more time to grow.

Persona: Ones see the flaws in themselves and the world around them. They are the fixers of humankind. The little imperfections nag at them, and it's often hard for a One to let things go. You can see how this can be a good thing and a bad thing. When it manifests as perfectionism, it can drive the One (and everyone around her) insane in short order. But when the One consciously expresses this through something like satire, her social commentary can help readers feel *less* crazy by seeing that someone else notices the hypocrisy and nonsense of the status quo. These natural impulses of the One can also be used to project a persona of strong integrity through summoning up the moral courage to call out inequality and unfairness in the world... and then doing something about it. Smart Ones rally their fans for causes they believe in, and this creates a strong community who feel like better people when they unite with their favorite author. Pretty powerful stuff.

Themes: As discussed in the previous chapter, the One might tend toward themes of justice, equality, imperfection, righteousness, belonging, goodness, evil, loneliness, responsibility, growth, acceptance (especially self-acceptance).

Protagonists: Type 1 protagonists are hot right now, so there's no financial reason to divert from this comfy territory. In a world full of hypocrisy, corruption, and misinformation, the public is starved for the wisdom, clarity, and integrity of Ones who call out what is wrong and aren't afraid to get their hands dirty trying to clean it up. So our Reformer author decides to stick to her strengths and write these types of characters who align with her mission to make the world a better place.

EXAMPLE TYPE 2 CAREER

Creative Values: Twos are focused on earning love through giving help and are afraid they will prove unworthy of love, because of the nature of their core fear and core desire. This can lead to Twos going beyond the line of helping into enabling as a means of ingratiating themselves to others. The result is that the Two loses touch with their sense for how much help people require, and this inevitably leads to emotional burnout if not put in check. If a Two does not develop boundaries around their energy, their career faces serious danger of never getting off the ground.

It's hard to keep your business running when you're going in fifty directions doing everything for everyone else in your life. That's why it's crucial for Twos to construct a clear, aligned purpose for their career that satisfies their core desire in a deep and meaningful way. Unless the Two is mindful about where he gets his love supply, he will go for the quick fix of helping those who don't necessarily need his help rather than building something meaningful for his readers.

How this translates to a career strategy is that a Two might prioritize reader interaction or building a fan community so he can stay plugged into how much help and healing he's providing his readers through the delayed gratification of publishing books. He intentionally crafts his stories to heal and nurture his readers, to be a place where readers can come to be cared for and experience unconditional love through the lives of his characters. This purpose creates a healthy and fulfilling career for him that he's happy to spend more of his time nurturing.

Persona: Twos are absolutely the shoulder to cry on and the one who shows up with the casserole when someone is struggling. There's no reason why our Two author shouldn't let this caring nature shine through his persona. This doesn't mean he doesn't set boundaries; in fact, setting boundaries becomes even more necessary of a skill to maintain this persona. But it means that he encourages his community to show up for each other. He highlights random acts of kindness, show readers that everyone is deserving of love, and when he could use some help himself, he does the scariest thing for him and *asks for it*. Even after all the love a Two has given, he'll be shocked to see how much his readers are eager to give in return.

Themes: As discussed in the previous chapter, the Two might tend toward themes of responsibility, connection, pride, family, love, worth, helping/enabling, identity, individualism, generosity, boundaries.

Protagonists: There aren't a lot of Two protagonists to be found out there, and once you understand the type, you start to see why: a Two's tendency to neglect their own needs and spend their energy fulfilling the needs of those around them doesn't always bring "main character" energy. Instead, we see a lot of Twos playing the literal "helper" secondary character. Our Two author sees this and understands that there's a *huge* hole in the market for Two protagonists, and nobody better to write them than him. For inspiration of how a Two can steal the spotlight, our author need look no further than Dolly Parton, who has become a national treasure through her generous heart. Bringing the Helper protagonist out of their usual supporting role and moving them front and center will help readers to do the same in their lives. It aligns perfectly with the kind of self-love this author wants to share with his readers.

EXAMPLE TYPE 3 CAREER

Creative values: Threes want to bring value to the world and avoid being seen as worthless by others, as shaped by their core motivations. The trouble starts when the Three searches for what *others* value and tries to shape her life to fit it. This is a game with no end, since different people value different accomplishments, and no person can do it all. For a Three caught up in this game, every achievement she hasn't reached can feel like points off her worth. But there's nothing wrong with the Achiever's desire to deliver value to the world, and if she works on some of these Enneagram patterns to unwind them, she can do great things without disconnecting from her own creative values to accomplish what she set out to do. A Three with a clear goal in mind and a plan for execution is a powerful thing.

How she translates this into her career strategy is that the Three shifts her goal from *earning* value to inspiring others to understand their inherent value. Threes are inspirational by nature, so shifting from the attitude of "please approve of me" into the authentic role model is the turning point of this type. But it starts by admitting openly to the one thing Threes hate the most: failure.

Our example author decides that she wants to inspire the world through her stories to live messy and pursue failures in chasing one's dreams. But also to learn *what* those dreams are and to shake off the goals imposed upon one by others. She knows that spending her money to encourage readers to chase their dreams will fill her up more than any flashy purchase, and so that's where the money flows (after bills and a few indulgences, of course). And finally, because she understands that she's extra susceptible to the allure of playing the slot machine of indie publishing, she builds an honest group of other committed authors to help her avoid the shiny bait and stay focused on her long-term goals.

Persona: Our Three will naturally accomplish whatever she sets out to do—there's no question about that. When your core desire is to deliver value and that translates to "being the best" or "coming out on top," you naturally develop an eye for opportunities and learn how to squeeze the most out of the established system. But this author has already decided that she doesn't want to play the game of constantly being "on" and performing for those around her. She wants to show her authentic self. So that's what she'll do through her outward-facing author presence. She'll share her failures along the path to success and talk about her battle to stay in touch with her innate value. She'll inspire her readers to chase their dreams, both flashy and not, and pause to check in with themselves, rather than engaging in nonstop action for a distraction. If our Three needs a role model for how to do this, she can look at Oprah (3w2) or Taylor Swift (3w4) and the way they've build their empires and fandoms through hard work, tears, failures, and dreams they just can't give up.

Themes: As discussed in the previous chapter, the Three might tend toward themes of worth, happiness, contentment, success, support, vanity, status, connection, acceptance, significance.

Protagonists: Because our Three author is naturally enamored with glitz and glam, she decides to write stories that take place among the rich and famous. Her protagonists are like her—chasing dreams, searching for value in all the wrong places—and at the start of their stories, they fall into the same traps that every Three is susceptible to. They are striving, but perhaps they haven't been in the driver's seat about what they're striving *for*. The inciting incident for Achiever protagonists is almost always that they either achieve what they set out for and it feels hollow, or (more likely) they've failed to achieve what they set out for, and their life falls apart. She writes about a lawyer who's passed up for a promotion and fired and must return to her small town to lick her wounds. She writes about a magical prince whose father banishes him and passes the crown to the next in line. And through these protagonists, she shows her readers that failure isn't the end, but instead merely the beginning of a much greater tale.

EXAMPLE TYPE 4 CAREER

Creative values: Fours are focused on their place in the world and how to be uniquely themselves, since that's what their core motivations are about. This can lead to a feeling of being misunderstood, which actually serves them insofar as it indicates that they *are* unique—but it ultimately keeps them miserable. This inner conflict can spill over into their writing if they're not careful, manifesting as stories that fit no particular genre and are complicated to the point of being incomprehensible. As you might imagine, these books are tricky to market. But once the Four decides that they are *already* unique and significant, they can let go of the need to feel misunderstood and strive for being understood instead. They start to embrace genre and tropes as a means of smooth communication between author and reader, understanding that they can remain unique and highly creative in their use of those tools.

How this translates to a career strategy is that the Four has realized he is not the only one feeling the way he does, and he wants to create stories that explore his deep well of emotions and show readers who feel the same natural sense of unnamable longing that they have company along the lonely road. He understands that he can't help but be different, so he stops putting his energy toward being even *more* eccentric and instead focuses that energy on a disciplined writing practice. Books that never get written can't find the readers who need them, after all.

The trick for this author is to stay focused on that goal of finding the lost ones and letting them know there's nothing broken about them just because they don't fit in. That way, he can remain alert to the reality that storytelling conventions are there to help unique communication stay intelligible rather than to create conformity, and that being as absolutely unusual as possible is not the hill he wants to die on. It's also important for him to remember that money from his creations isn't an indicator of him selling out, but rather a resource that allows him to continue expressing himself creatively.

Persona: Fours are going to be quirky; there's no way around it. This author doesn't even need to try. But he also understands that his nature can lead him to slip into envy and self-loathing, so he's mindful about not connecting with his readers when he's in the midst of those moods. He understands that sharing authentically about it *after* the fact can spark healing in readers who often feel the same and believe there's something wrong with them for it, but he knows that sharing *about* moods and sharing moods is not the same thing, so he's watchful.

Writing is not his only creative pursuit, and he shares the others with his readers to show that humans can't help but create and that there's value in creating for the sake of creating, even if the result is weird or unskilled and could never be turned for a profit. Maybe *especially* if that's the case. In developing this authentic persona, he builds a community of artists and oddballs who feel like they've finally found their people.

Themes: As discussed in the previous chapter, the Four might tend toward themes of purpose, identity, envy, loneliness, dependence, spirit, aspiration, dreams, addiction, obsession, significance, authenticity.

Protagonists: Fours are identity seekers, and their protagonists tend to be the same. This author decides to write stories about protagonists who are searching for the truth of who they are, craving the knowledge even as they fear a clear definition might stifle their spirit. He writes stories of the outcast who turns out to be The Chosen One, whose unique powers once left her rejected but are now the only thing that can save the universe. He writes protagonists who thrive only through their ragtag band of misfit friends and who can see the bittersweet beauty in the world, even as it's falling apart.

EXAMPLE TYPE 5 CAREER

Creative values: Fives are focused on gaining skills and knowledge as a way of meeting their core motivations around competency and capability. But this desire to learn can turn into a need to already know, if the Five is not mindful about it, and nothing kills the drive for learning faster than the belief that one already knows. For this reason, Fives are often reluctant to share their knowledge, fearing that someone will point out a flaw. But the fastest way to greater knowledge is stress-testing current understanding by sharing with others, not keeping it locked away.

How this translates to a career strategy is that our Five might decide she wants to share the process of her learning through her writing. She wants to bring out the curiosity in others while also being paid enough to continue her own intellectual pursuits. The search for truth will be at the forefront of her stories, and she'll decide upon settings and character occupations based on what she hopes to learn more about.

Persona: The Five has decided that she will proceed mindfully about the *learning vs. knowing* challenge of her type and present herself to her readers as a seeker rather than an expert. She may very well be an expert in certain subjects, but readers can figure that out on their own. The Five knows that she wants to inspire that curiosity and passion for learning for others, so she models it rather than using her position as the author to score ego points for her current knowledge. When she doesn't know the answer to something yet, she asks her readers what they think of it or if they have any knowledge to share. She joyfully shares with her readers her many adventures in the pursuit of the facts and accuracy she includes in her books.

Themes: As discussed in the previous chapter, the Five might tend toward themes of truth, reality, avarice, memory, loneliness, exploration, respect, independence, self-sufficiency, abundance/scarcity.

Protagonists: The Five's protagonists are knowledge seekers because this allows her to follow her own passion of learning in the process of writing them. It also inspires her readers to be knowledge seekers, which builds a community of intellectuals around her books who share facts and don't get too caught up in sharing feelings—exactly the type of community where the Five feels at home. She writes protagonists who struggle with the fear of not yet knowing and who explore the various *types* of knowledge beyond the mere intellectual—archeologists, librarians, private investigators. Through her protagonists, she builds a safe place to tackle her hardest subject matter yet: reconnecting with her heart and instinct.

EXAMPLE TYPE 6 CAREER

Creative values: Sixes are focused on support and security as a result of their core motivations. This Six has decided to respect that in himself by committing to a slow and steady approach to his career. He understands that he can experience a massive fight-or-flight response to instability or too much dependence on a single source of income, and he's not going to try to "push through" that for the promise of fast cash. Instead, he's building his author platform across multiple retailers, understanding that this strategy is a marathon, not a sprint. While he knows his life runs more smoothly when he has money tucked away in an emergency fund, he's also consciously investing back into his business so that it can grow and provide further security in the future.

Sixes are drawn toward group projects, and he leverages collaboration to grow his business, but he also understands that under stress he's prone to expecting too much loyalty from others and accusing allies of being enemies when they show that their individual business interests ultimately come first. So he manages his expectations of others in his beneficial collaborations and focuses on what he's gained that he otherwise might've missed out on.

Persona: Gathering others to them is a natural talent for the Six, and so he creates an accessible meeting place for his readers to gather. But while he's invested in his reader community, he also knows that seeking external security or "safety in numbers" is a sign that he's lost touch with his internal authority and needs to take a step back to reconnect with himself. In taking this mindful approach, he's able to keep the culture of the group focused on collaboration rather than "us vs. them" thinking. He aligns the group in such a way that they support his growth rather than encouraging his stress response.

Themes: As discussed in the previous chapter, the Six might tend toward themes of loyalty, responsibility, trust, fear, authority, security, connection, abandonment, support, reliance, courage.

Protagonists: Sixes can't help but write protagonists who are as in touch with their sense of fear as the author who created them. This Six decides he's going to flow with this energy rather than fighting against it, and his protagonists always find themselves up against huge external threats that can only be overcome with courage and collaboration. But they're also no stranger to betrayal, and by roleplaying his nightmare, the Six creates a safe environment in which to play out the worst-case scenario and learn all the ways that he could still be okay in the face of it.

EXAMPLE TYPE 7 CAREER

Creative values: Sevens are focused on freedom and satisfaction as a result of their core motivations. This can lead to a reputation of "always being a good time" or "being a flake." But our Seven author has decided that she's going to leverage her gifts of freedom and joy to her advantage. Since she likes variety (but knows that there's such a thing as splitting her focus in too many directions), she's decided to build out two series in unlike genres at the same time. When she gets bored of one, she already has another to hop over to for a book or two. It's the perfect balance to gain traction without feeling locked into one route.

She leverages the money she earns from her books to travel on research trips (and works with her accountant to claim the appropriate tax write-offs). First, she decides where she wants to travel, then she decides how to work it into her books. As a result, readers flock to her books for rich and luxurious details from her adventures.

Persona: Though Sevens often struggle in their personal relationships because of their reluctance to work through the ugly parts of life with others, for her readers, she gets to play the part of the fun best friend, the nomadic aunt, the adrenaline junky. When readers need a hilarious tale or an emotional pick-me-up, they check in with her stories and know they're in for a treat. When the world seems like it's falling apart, our Seven holds a space where fun, joy, and optimism are still possible, and her readers reward her for that in sales and enthusiastic word of mouth.

Themes: As discussed in the previous chapter, the Seven might tend toward themes of joy, pain, fear, avoidance, reality, contentment, responsibility, faith, satisfaction, freedom, abundance/scarcity.

Protagonists: Because this Seven wants to be on the move, she writes her protagonists to match her energy level. They travel, hunt for treasure, or accept jobs in faraway lands. But they also find themselves unmoored from time to time, wishing for a companion to spend their life with or a place to call home. Sometimes they feel like they can never squeeze enough out of life, and the search for the next best thing is starting to wear on them. And sometimes, their external freedom is taken away from them completely, and they must figure out how to manage. She writes stories about protagonists who learn the difference between pleasure and enjoyment, who find the value in gratitude, and who are forced to confront those ugly feelings they've been trying to outrun. And through this process, our Seven learns to appreciate the world around her, even if she's staying in one familiar location.

EXAMPLE TYPE 8 CAREER

Creative values: Eights want to feel in control and strong as a result of their core motivations. This is something to both respect and keep an eye on in their business. This Eight is in his element as an indie author, getting to call all the shots creatively and business-wise. He's keenly aware that the good Amazon giveth, but the good Amazon also taketh away—often without any opportunity for recourse—and that power imbalance doesn't sit well with him. So he builds his business across multiple retailers, understanding that if any single one tries to exert unjust power over him, he can simply leave and never look back. To maintain even more control over his platform, he focuses on direct sales from his website so that he owns that traffic and tracking.

Eights are born to lead, so it's a natural step for him to bring on a few people to help manage the platform while he continues to write. He understands the difference between *power over* and *empowerment* and has been careful to hire the right people so he can empower all his hires to handle their work without needing approval for everything they do. With the money that he earns, he pays his assistants fairly and saves responsibly to create a cushion so he can leave any situation where the power imbalance has become unfavorable to him.

Persona: Because Eights are naturally what-you-see-is-what-you-get to the point of brutal honesty, this Eight's persona reflects that without even trying. What he focuses on instead is making sure that his need to challenge comes from a place of protecting those who are vulnerable rather than needing to prove he's strong and untouchable. This Eight also knows that real strength is found through *accepting* vulnerability, and he's not afraid to show that feeling fear, loneliness, and all the other unpleasant-but-necessary human emotions isn't a sign of weakness, but rather evidence of how strong we are to keep fighting despite our vulnerabilities.

Themes: As discussed in the previous chapter, the Eight might tend toward themes of courage, vulnerability, control, power, responsibility, kindness, destiny, conflict, significance, strength, leadership.

Protagonists: Eights tend to write protagonists who are daring, natural leaders, and courageous fighters for the little guy, whether the author mean to or not. This is just who the Eight is, and they have a hard time understanding why more people are not. These bold protagonists and their connection to their own inner authority will attract readers who wish they could feel so sure of themselves in a complicated world. As the Eight author learns their type's virtue of kindness and adds that into their protagonists' DNA, these main characters will transcend from invigorating to legendary.

EXAMPLE TYPE 9 CAREER

Creative values: Nines are focused on harmony and peace as a result of their core motivations. They prefer to maintain a gentle balance in their work life and not rock the boat or push themselves too hard. Because of their conflict-avoidant tendencies, Nines can ignore problems until they become bigger than they need to be and unavoidable. This Nine knows that to preserve harmony in her writing life, she must address the problems in her personal life as they arise, rather than putting them off. This Nine uses her gifts of seeing things from all angles to create rich, character-driven stories that act as a safe place to practice working through conflicts that seem insurmountable. By using this gift of diplomacy, she satisfies her internal need to create harmony and shows the world that no relationship is too damaged to repair if all parties are committed to it.

When she finds that her writing motivation is lacking, she understands that she's likely disconnecting from herself as a way of avoiding a conflict that she doesn't want to address. Because she cares so deeply about her writing, she addresses the situation so she can reconnect with herself and her creative energy.

Persona: This Nine believes that there's strength in diversity. At the same time, she sees the commonalities between individuals more than the differences, and she expresses that to her readers in such a way that all feel welcome. She builds an online home for her readers and assigns assertive but respectful moderators to it to address conflict directly so that her energy isn't sapped by playing mediator all the time. She understands that ignoring conflict may feel like preserving peace, but when it comes to settling issues, the only meaningful way out is through. She also understands that as a deeply sensitive individual, she doesn't need to be the one inserting herself into every conflict that will arise in her community.

Themes: As discussed in the previous chapter, the Nine might tend toward themes of serenity, conflict, action, loneliness, connection/disconnection, avoidance, courage, responsibility, harmony, belonging, identity, significance.

Protagonists: This Nine writes protagonists who don't feel like their gifts are valued by the world or that their voice and their opinions matter. Then she puts them in a situation where their gifts are the only thing that can save the day. Her quiet and thoughtful protagonists will show how the world is never black and white but a full spectrum of color, and they will almost always be surrounded by a diverse and supportive group of allies to help them along. By doing this, the Nine's stories will show the peaceful path forward in a world full of pain and conflict.

Remember, these are just examples for each type. Within each of the nine types is an array of individuals whose strategy must also be informed by past experience, skills and strengths, and current life situation. Not all Type 6s will make the same decisions, for instance, and nor should they. But as long as we respect the core motivations that drive us as we design our career, we can mindfully build an aligned path that keeps us growing, fulfilled, and excited to continue on.

THAT'S HOW IT'S DONE

This, folks, is how you build an aligned career. You must anchor yourself in something that is not money, because money ebbs and flows. Start with something meaningful to you, something unchanging about who you are at your core.

I hope you've gained clarity not only on your purpose for taking on this super-challenging career, but also how you can advance that purpose through your stories.

If you're treating indie publishing like a sprint, you're going to run out of steam. That's not to say you can't show up with passion and intensity on more days than not. But a marathon isn't merely a bunch of back-to-back sprints. It requires a different strategy.

If I've accomplished what I set out to do, you're starting to envision your strategy more vividly and *feeling* it, too. You'll need your head, heart, and gut engaged for this massive and often uncharted endeavor. You don't need to reinvent the wheel, but you must decide upon the wheel that's right for you, because no one else can.

Armed with the Enneagram (and the continued self-learning you'll undoubtedly want to do after finishing this book), you now have a personalized framework that can serve as your criteria for making the right decisions as your career progresses.

Maybe you won't leave this book with a clear to-do list of *tactics*, but those are just details that change daily, growing and waning in effectiveness at breakneck speed. While others jump from one tactic to the other, trying everything they can and running themselves into the ground, you'll now be able to easily evaluate the hot new tactic and understand if it supports your goals and your soul or not. Maybe, if you feel in a generous spirit, you'll tell those tired trend-chasers about this book.

Thank you for joining me on this pet project of mine. If you found this book helpful, please leave it a review on your retailer of choice. If you didn't find it helpful, feel free to ignore the last sentence.

In all seriousness, I would love to see a new wave of indies building sustainable and fulfilling careers in lieu of prospecting and get-rich-quick schemes. That's my ideal environment in which to continue growing my own fiction career, because in that industry, each person is confident in the value that their gifts bring. In that industry, there's no backstabbing, sabotaging, and cutthroat competition. We're all walking alongside each other. If a reader doesn't like your books, if the gifts you offer aren't appreciated, you don't take it personally—you simply recommend them to an indie author they *would* enjoy, no hard feelings.

Doesn't that sound nice? Doesn't that sound like an industry, a *community*, you would be proud to call your own? Let's build it together, and we start by looking and listening and loving internally, by focusing on what we truly desire and what we have to offer. Now more than ever, the world needs all of us tapping into our gifts. We are storytellers, and stories are the only thing that have ever and will ever change hearts and minds. We have the power to shape the world. How do you want it to look?

ALIGNMENT IS A PROCESS, NOT A DESTINATION

My sincere hope is that after reading this book and working through some of the chapter questions you'll feel empowered to continue exploring these concepts on your own for a long time. The point of the Enneagram is self-exploration and self-connection, after all. That's all it is, a framework of emotional language to help you connect more fully to yourself so that you can then connect more fully and authentically with the world around you.

The more that I learn to love my unique construction and to appreciate and respect what motivates me, the more I appreciate the differences I find in others. There is no one total-package person who has everything and can do everything. When we learn to appreciate the benefits of our core desires and what those desires naturally draw us toward, we're better able to appreciate that others are drawn toward other things, and by working with the right people who bring complementary gifts, we can achieve incredible results.

You may ask at this point, "Where do I go from here?"

I love me some actionable items, so I feel you on this.

The problem, of course, is that the best way to apply these concepts will look different from person to person. There's no universally correct answer here. My goal was to give you tools to approach your career, and self-knowledge that will help you make the right decisions for your life.

This book contains a lot of information, and you may have to read it multiple times or at various points in your career as you work to fully incorporate the practices.

But in a general sense, here are some things that I suggest you do to reclaim your author career.

First, set aside time to churn over what we've discussed and see what comes up for you. And by that, I don't mean *at some point* when you *magically have free time*. I mean pull up your calendar right now and schedule one or two hours this week or next. Use that time to reflect on and write down what parts of your author business are not in alignment with your creative values, your persona, your themes, and your protagonists. (If you've answered the chapter questions already, those will be a valuable reference for this.) And then when that scheduled reflection time arrives, don't treat it as optional. If the task before it on your calendar takes longer than expected, don't eat into the reflection time. Move it back or reschedule for the next available date (but keep pushing it back, back, back to your own detriment).

Reflecting, strategizing, and *planning* the execution of your aligned career is the most effective use of your time as a business owner.

If you can, move all electronics out of your reach, or better yet the room, while you complete your reflection time. I also recommend pouring yourself a nice hot drink, taking a few deep belly breaths, and maybe whispering some sweet nothings to yourself as a reminder that you are deserving of this quiet mental space.

Then allow yourself to *think*, to lose track of time, to reflect on how your core fears and core desires have led you blindly thus far and what your business would look like if you worked mindfully with them rather than at their bidding.

From that free write, my favorite thing to do is to take an honest inventory of everything I can *stop* doing or hand off to someone else because it doesn't hit on my emotional needs.

You may realize over the course of this exercise that you already possess enough industry knowledge to proceed with your new vision. If that's the case, one of the things you might be able to cut out, for instance, is indie author Facebook groups and publishing podcasts (yes, even Sell More Books Show). Inputs like these can be a firehose of information, and if you don't need them, then they are more than likely just distractions that are providing instant gratification to your core desire or temporarily drowning out your core fear.

These types of tactics-based resources, while helpful at various stages of your career, can also lead you into the temptation of "This one thing worked well for this one person, so I should drop everything I'm doing and try it for some quick money."

If you find, in this reflection time, that you know what you need to know, then it's time to put that into practice.

What you could also discover during your reflection time is that you *don't* yet have the complete knowledge to accomplish your vision, in which case your action item might be defining *what* knowledge you need to gain. You'll have a much better idea of that once you complete this free write and reflection, and then you can seek the specific information and avoid getting carried away in the vast possibilities.

Or maybe you realize that you don't know everything... but it's time to start anyway. In an industry like ours, sometimes you *can't* know everything until you try a few things yourself. This is the first nonfiction book I've written. There was so much I didn't know about this process prior to starting, but when I tuned in, I felt it in my bones that it was time to dive in, ready or not. I'm glad I did, because if I'd waited until I knew how to do this, I probably would've put it off indefinitely.

Secondly, if you find you don't know how to do specific things, you can ask for help. If you've created a network of indie authors you trust, now might be the time to reach out to one and say, "Hey, I see that you're doing well with this specific thing. It's something that I need to do more of in my business. Is there a time when you could show me a few tricks to get me started?" Don't expect this kind of energy from people you sorta know through Facebook or have only chatted with once and briefly, and don't ask it of people who are experts in the subject matter and offer a book or paid coaching and consulting. They've put a price on their knowledge, and it's best to respect that and pay them for it. But for the people you've developed relationships with and whom you believe you have something to offer in return, go for it. Don't ask, "How do I get your successful career?" Instead ask, "How did you do this one thing so well?"

Then always, *always* filter their response through your new decision-making criteria to make sure it works for you and your creative values.

ADDITIONAL RESOURCES FOR THE COMMITTED AUTHOR

If you want a guide to walk you through the specific concepts we've discussed in this book, I offer a ton of resources, both free and paid, for authors like you.

I offer one-on-one consulting for both your story and your career and two courses for supercharging your fiction. I also co-host a weekly podcast with Bryan Cohen called Sell More Books Show, wherein an Enneagram One (me) and a Three (Bryan) tap into our industry experience to discuss how to use the current publishing system to your absolute advantage... while also staying ethical and true to yourself. You can find more information on that, plus links to my YouTube channel and blog, at www.ffs.media/resources.

THE ALIGNED AUTHOR

An aligned author feels calm and confident about their career. They make decisions based on clear criteria of their money motivations and writing motivations rather than functioning on instant gratification or a fear-avoidance response on a day-to-day basis. They either know what their next big move is, or they don't but they're not worried about it because they trust that they will know it when they see it.

An aligned author has other authors and public figures and friends whom they look up to and admire, but they don't try to *be* those people. An aligned author isn't trying to be anyone but their most liberated self.

However, that doesn't mean they overidentify with their type and develop a fixed mindset. An aligned author is always growing. They aren't defining themselves rigidly as a means of avoiding growth, in a petulant "this is just who I am" kind of way. They are learning to better understand their core motivations to connect with their true self and define an appropriate growth path. And then they are actively pursuing that growth, knowing how uncomfortable and messy the process can be.

An aligned author is not concerned with the success of others, outside of helping them celebrate it. The more we learn about ourselves, the more we realize how individualized success looks and that, no matter what, another person's success was never ours to have. It is no statement on us, we were never entitled to it, so all that's left for us to do is help them embrace it.

An aligned author understands that there are other publishing paths that they may not agree with because not everyone shares their core motivations. As a result, an aligned author does not involve themselves in author community drama. Drama doesn't align with any healthy Enneagram type. It is the ultimate energy waster and a sure sign of our own discontent. An aligned author may take a stand when morally compelled to do so but will always consider first whether they are using it as an opportunity to be righteous and courageous (a sign of health) or self-righteous and performative (both unhealthy behaviors).

An aligned author has a long, steady career ahead of them if they so choose. When we are aligned with our core motivations and have clear creative values that we hold ourselves to, our individual success is guaranteed because we are successful simply by embracing ourselves. That said, aligned authors may need to extend their timeline further than expected before seeing the external results they'd hoped for, but the ultimate point of alignment is never the external results—it's that we enjoy the ride regardless of results we cannot control. Being aligned with your purpose in your creative pursuit is a daily success story.

An aligned author regularly falls out of alignment. Misalignment is part of being human and living within groups and societies with competing values to our own. Our needs as social creatures often encourage us to compromise, but an aligned author learns how to recognize the signs of severe misalignment and is committed to getting back on track.

There isn't a finish line for alignment because it is a practice. There's no point at which we permanently transcend temptation to conform and become a big, glowing ball of light. So long as we continue to need food and shelter and friends, we will always be pulled back in.

And I think that's great. Because each time we regain our temporary alignment, we appreciate it more than we did before. We may even feel like we're flying. But you can't achieve that high without the preceding low.

That's why, as an aligned author, you won't beat yourself up when you lose touch with your heart, mind, and instincts. Instead, you'll simply celebrate each time that you get to find yourself again.

The End

NOTES

2. WHAT ARE THE NINE TYPES?

1. Teaching the process of moving from reacting to responding is beyond the scope of this book, but it essentially relies upon increased self-knowledge (which you'll gain in these pages) and building a strong mindfulness practice. If this is a skill you would love to work on, there are fabulous books on mindfulness, and part of the fun is finding the one that speaks to you.
2. The surest bet is the one offered on the Enneagram Institute website, which currently costs $12. Totally worth it if you can swing it, y'all. If not, I also like the one on Crystal Knows and Eclectic Energies.
3. An entry-level read: *The Road Back to You: An Enneagram Journey to Self-Discovery* by Ian Morgan Cron and Susanne Stabile

   More in-depth breakdowns of the types: *The Wisdom of the Enneagram: The Complete Guide to Psychological and Spiritual Growth for the Nine Personality Types* by Don Richard Riso and Russ Hudson

3. WHAT ARE MY CREATIVE VALUES?

1. The fact that this whole book isn't quotes from *The Princess Bride* is a massive show of restraint from me.

ACKNOWLEDGMENTS

I can say with certainty that I never would've gotten my ass in gear on this book were it not for the generous support and encouragement from the *Reclaim Your Author Career* Kickstarter backers.

Thank you to all the backers, and a special shout out to:

Amanda Cashure, Anmarie Uber, B. LaMotte, Becca Syme, Bryan Cohen, Casey Griffin, Cathy Peper, Charlene Perry, Clara Woods, Danielle Corley, Danielle Staley, Emme Grange, Gillian St. Kevern, Jamie Davis, Jan Field, Jeff King, Jeffrey Griffith, Jesse Friedman, Jim Graziano, Josee Smith, Julie Burch, Justin Stewart, Kara Jaden, Katrina Marie, Kevin Crowell, Krystal Shannan, Lily Cahill, Lisa-Marie Cabrelli, Lorraine Johnston, M. A. Brave, Martha Carr, Mary Lynn Mercer, MJ Silversmith, Mom :), Monica Leonelle, Natascha Birovljev, Patti, Rob Falla, Rona Gofstein, Ryan Schroeder, Sarah R., Scott Walker, Sonia Manzo, Tameri Etherton, Taryn Elliott, Trixie Silvertale, Xavier Champagne, and Zoe Cannon

I'm also indebted to Monica Leonelle and Russell Nohelty for sharing their hard-earned knowledge about how to run a successful Kickstarter. That being said, please take a vacation, you two.

OneMind also deserves a mention for cheering me on during those weeks when I thought about a career change then realized I didn't have any other marketable skills. This group was also the incubator for my rekindled interest in the Enneagram, and that's clearly had its impact on me and my brain, for better or worse.

Were it not for Bryan Cohen, I would've named this book something stupid and unmarketable. Bryan Cohen? More like Bryan *Knowin'* how to name a book, amirite?

Thank you to Alyssa Archer for being a wonderful editor of this and many of my other books. Your diplomatic comments when I've made a complete shit salad of words are always greatly appreciated.

Lastly, always, to John. As you wish.

ABOUT CLAIRE TAYLOR

Claire Taylor is an independent author and the owner of FFS Media. She offers courses, coaching, and consulting for writers who want to supercharge their fiction and align their career.

She still lives in her hometown of Austin, Texas.

Find her author services and fiction at www.ffs.media.

To receive tips and tricks to make your next story unforgettable, sign up for the FFS Media Story Nerds: www.ffs.media/join.

Milton Keynes UK
Ingram Content Group UK Ltd.
UKHW022227130624
444044UK00006BA/136

9 781959 041016